Christina Fischer

MAKING SENSE OF FOOD & WINE

Concepts for Combinations

Christina Fischer

MAKING SENSE OF FOOD & WINE
Concepts for Combinations

Edition
Fackelträger

Contents

Making Sense of Food & Wine: Concepts for Combinations

The pleasurable combination of wine and food has long been an integral part of my life. Eventually, however, I reached the point where I wanted to know why some combinations worked especially well, while others didn't. Up until this time, my findings were based largely on personal experience. I had only a few logical explanations and yet these were not found in relevant literature on the subject. With some helpful support and food chemistry basics, I went to the bottom of these findings and tried to define them in a way that was easy to understand. That was the starting point for the first edition of *Making Sense of Food & Wine* which you now, in a comprehensively revised and expanded form, have before you. The result is a systematic guide which clearly explains the alliance between wine and food but, much as it is scientific, doesn't leave out pleasure.

Enjoyment is a wonderful, but highly individual, experience which is perceived by all of our senses. So also is taste, which not only describes the scientific reaction taking place on the tongue, but also includes a subjective perception which varies from person to person. Taste is conditioned by such things as family upbringing, cultural differences, national customs, and, last but not least, by one's social environment.

This is reason enough to want to know more about our sensations and the complex sense of "taste." How does taste function? Sure, we all know that you "eat with your eyes first," that aroma molecules get sniffed out, and that basic taste characteristics are identified by receptors on the tongue which are also supported by different stimuli and textures. But which role do aromas play in this game? Perhaps one could liken their intensity with a stereo's volume control: loud or faint. Then there is the exciting interaction between sweetness, acidity, bitterness, saltiness, umami, texture and fat. Is the palate stimulated by acidity or bitterness, or is it coated by sweetness or a layer of fat? On top of that, all of these parameters can also be altered by different cooking methods. A filet of beef tastes differently, depending on whether it is fried, grilled, poached or served raw.

What's more, we live in a globalized world, and every day we're confronted with very diverse culinary influences and products. With the international wine market's ever-changing variety of choices, finding our bearings is further complicated. The situation is similarly complex with different cooking styles, foods and ingredients. When both come together, the implications are quite complex.

At this point, you shouldn't be daunted with intimidation, but rather continue reading with curiosity. What follows is a systematic examination of the pleasurable interaction between wine and food, from a logical classification of wine types to easy-to-understand rules for everyday use. This book provides a simple introduction to a complex subject. Not a dogmatic philosophy or an all-encompassing solution, but rather a guide for experimentation.

You'll soon discover that the world of tasting pleasure is not a book of seven seals. To navigate between the poles of personal experience and scientific knowledge, what is needed is merely a dose of common sense, a pinch of sensitivity, and an insatiable desire for something new. With this book, you can have the confidence to gradually tackle this subject, sip-by-sip. And because it isn't just about wine, but also about food, it inevitably leads to a passion with a system–but under the premise that taste is not bound by rules. So do as you like.

Yours,
Christina Fischer

A Gastronomic

Revolution

A Gastronomic Revolution

Good, Plain Cooking Versus Nouvelle Cuisine

At the start of the 1970s a new culinary era in Europe was dawning. An almost revolutionary change took place, from rich, filling meals to exquisite culinary experiences. One of the most important pioneers of this delicious trend was the Austrian chef Eckart Witzigmann. His culinary career began in 1971 in Munich's "Tantris" restaurant, after he completed a formative apprenticeship period with the great French masters Paul Bocuse and Paul Haeberlin. He was the first German-speaking chef to receive the highly coveted three-Michelin-star rating for his own restaurant, "Aubergine." According to Wolfram Siebeck, Germany's most critical palate, there are contemporaries who divide their culinary experiences into two different time periods: "pre-Witzigmann" and "post-Witzigmann."

If one looks at the culinary landscape during the "pre-Witzigmann" years, this statement certainly seems comprehensible. Apart from the gastronomic establishments in Germany's southwestern regions close to France such as the Erbprinzen in Ettlingen, the Ritter in Durbach and the Schwarzer Adler in Oberbergen, most restaurants at that time served home-style dishes. Many a tender piece of meat fell victim to heavy gravy. Vegetables and potatoes were cooked beyond recognition in the same pot, while most of the time fish was boiled. And wine with a meal? Rather unlikely.

The concept of enjoying fresh, creative cuisine together with skillfully selected wines only meant something to those who, at the time, were regular travelers throughout France's gourmet circuit. For, at this time, a

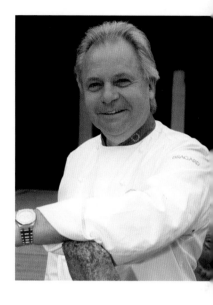

second revolution was taking place under the catch phrase "Nouvelle Cuisine."

This new cuisine was based on a food's freshness and intrinsic flavor. At the same time, special emphasis was placed on the visual appearance of individual dishes, and the art of food presentation became increasingly important. Witzigmann zealously adopted all of these ideas and trends, and taught an entire country that food can be something more than just sustenance.

The Gourmet World's First Pioneers

Witzigmann and his colleagues were not put off when dandelion greens were teasingly termed "rabbit food" and when, outside of France, some ingredients were hard to come by. All over the country, a culinary network was being established. In 1978 Karl-Heinz Wolf, an innovative restaurateur from Bonn, started a specialized wholesale food company called Rungis-Express, which supplied restaurants directly. In those early days, he regularly drove to Paris to stock up on fresh products which were not yet available in Germany. Adalbert Schmitt, with his restaurant "Schweizer Stuben" is also among the first pioneers. In 1972, he hired Jörg Müller (a native of Baden working in Switzerland at the time) as chef of a cuisine more oriented toward fresh ingredients.

Hans-Peter Wodarz and "old hand" Lothar Eiermann were also involved in this revolution. In the following years, Wodarz coined the term "gourmet theater." Even iconic French chefs such as Jean-Claude Bourgueil were drawn to Germany during this period. A circle of creative minds including Gerhard Gärtner, Vincent Klink,

Egbert Engelhardt and Harald Wohlfahrt belonged to the culinary revolutions of this age. They were the leading masterminds of a new culinary culture which evolved from modern French cuisine.

Countless connoisseurs wended their way to these restaurants, travelling long distances in order to eat well. These gourmet tourists did not, however, get offered German wine in the gourmet meccas of this era. Then, wine lists were dominated by French wines because they were considered especially compatible with food. Sommeliers knew each Bordeaux vine by name, yet–apart from a few prized Beeren- and Trockenbeerenauslesen–they did not know the name of a single top German wine.

This was understandable because, at the time, there was no improvement in quality, but rather a trend toward uniform standardized wines, which emanated from the wave of post-war sweet wines. This was an unfavorable development, for the more an average-quality wine exceeds a certain residual sugar threshold, the more it loses its identity.

In order for a wine to be a suitable food partner, it must have the right balance of components: fruit, acidity, sweetness and alcohol. Most winemakers might have produced dry wines if the combination of wine and food had had any significance at the time. However, in the 1970s, the majority of vintners too willingly embraced the standardized norm and thus were spared the effort of individual viticulture and winemaking.

People understood far too late
that most foods call for dry wines

The link between wine and food was more irrelevant than ever. This was mainly the case in cities which were far away from wine regions. Sommeliers and waitstaff could do nothing but to fetch Bordeaux, Chablis and Meursault and the like from their cellars. A short time later, it was understood that most foods call for dry wines. Regrettably, however, most winemakers responded to this demand by making unpalatable, acidulous wines. Because bone-dry, acidic Rieslings donning a "diabetic seal" (created especially for such wines) were far from enjoyable, restaurants continued to place their bets on foreign wines. But it got worse: Toward the end of the 1970s, Alsace's Edelzwicker became popular, with the emerging global player Chablis following in its footsteps. Then came Muscadet, Sancerre and Chardonnay. Even Pinot Grigio and Prosecco & Co. became cult beverages.

"Eating is now finally fun!"

Restaurants owed the 1980s emergence of good, dry German wines to several individual winemakers, such as Franz Keller from the Kaiserstuhl, Paul Schmitt in Franken (Franconia), Hans Rebholz from the Südpfalz (South Palatinate) and Hajo Becker from the Rheingau. Naturally, the burgeoning restaurant review trade played a part in this. The leading gourmet journalists Wolfram Siebeck, Gerd von Paczensky and Klaus Besser, as well as the wine writer Pit Falkenstein, were strong advocates for high quality, dry wines. The magazine *Essen & Trinken* was first published in the early 1970s, followed by *Feinschmecker* and Johann Willsberger's trendsetting magazine *Gourmet*, which reflected the spirit of the times both sensitively and creatively. In 1982, Willsberger's headline proclaimed: "Young chefs with new ideas, farm-fresh products, brave winemakers with dry wines: eating is now finally fun!" Suddenly, these winemakers who–against the trend–spent decades making dry wines and looking beyond their own cellar walls, advanced to stardom in the gourmet scene.

Combining Wine and Food

One of the most important masterminds of this time was Erwein Graf Matuschka-Greiffenclau, who, in 1977, took over the legacy of Schloss Vollrads in the Rheingau. The former Olivetti advertising manager confidently analyzed the market, and asked fundamental questions to find out why foreign wines were more successful than German wines, and why French wines were considered a perfect match for food.

Graf Matuschka painstakingly recorded the findings of his experiments

Together with Egbert Engelhardt (chef of the famous one-Michelin-star restaurant "Graues Haus" in Oestrich-Winkel), Matuschka-Greiffenclau compiled universal and, above all, comprehensible criteria for harmonious wine and food combinations. He kept meticulous written records of these findings and, since then, most of them have lost very little in relevance. Even if one might today wonder about some of the seemingly bold theories which, at the time, were probably formulated with a little too much personal enthusiasm for off-dry Riesling, Matuschka-Greiffenclau had achieved something exemplary for the German gastronomic scene. He led hundreds of culinary wine tastings in various restaurants as well as at Schloss Vollrads, entertaining a captivated audience with his witty speeches.

At the same time, in the South of Germany, Dr. Werner Schön contemplated the alliance of wine and food. He managed the Vintners' Association of Baden for 33 years and was miles ahead of his time. Together with Franz Keller and others, he was a significant protagonist in the change from a sweet, opulent Ruländer to a dry, elegant

Grauburgunder. This put important ideas into motion amongst vintners and winemakers and awakened the scene from its deep sleep.

The first market-driven vintner alliance of the 1980s, which included Michael Graf Adelmann, Armin Diel, Erwein Graf Matuschka-Greiffenclau and Dr. Carl von Schubert, emerged from all of these initiatives. Together they travelled the country, promoting German wine and its enjoyable liaison with good food. Matuschka-Greiffenclau's efforts, as well as those of many pioneers, provided the fundamental building blocks for today's culinary wine culture, which continues its exciting progress.

Present Day
Ambassadors of Culinary Pleasures

This is where contemporaries who are professionally devoted to the delicious alliance of wine and food have their say. All of them eat and drink with great pleasure. They link indulgent pleasures and culinary sensations with joie de vivre and time shared together.

It's not about expensive food, luxury goods or trends, but about the pure love of life and genuine products. It's about a steadfast resistance movement in a globalized consumer society which, unfortunately, no longer relies on its five senses and good judgement. A society much too influenced by the media environment, with its technicolor images and computerized superficialities, in which smell and taste play only a minor role. Smelling and tasting are sensitive sensations that threaten to atrophy under the influence of seemingly more exciting visual stimuli. Delicate nuanced aromas and sensual taste impressions are often powerless against the colorful seduction of our modern society. The daily stresses and strains, lack of time, and careless eating habits compound the situation. To "rely on one's own taste" has gained a different significance.

For this reason, it is both exciting and entertaining to read the personal views and individual remarks of our various epicurean advocates. They don't necessarily treat the subject of wine and food with seriousness, but rather with gastronomic enjoyment or, in some cases, pragmatism. There is not always a guarantee that the wine will match the food perfectly. Even experts can sometimes be influenced by their mood, and just do what they feel like doing. For them, it is more about a holistic way of living, and about the social value of eating and drinking together. This can culminate in situations of pure relaxation as well as lively conviviality.

For **Ingo Holland**, owner and creative mind behind the "Altes Gewürzamt" in Klingenberg, Germany, enjoyment means a slice of dark bread with French raw-milk butter and black Indian salt. He likes to pair this with a glass of dry rosé from Luberon or Bandol, preferably combined with ice cubes and sunshine.

He answers the question of whether wine should always go with the food straightforwardly: "No. I believe that the fun factor should be the ultimate priority. This doesn't mean that wine shouldn't be a harmonious match–rather, it means that the perfect wine and food match might have to take a back seat so that one can drink the wine one is in the mood for." You can tell that Holland does not just give thought to cooking, but also to the suitably matching wine. In recent years he has established himself as a specialist in the extensive world of spices, and he incessantly thinks up new ideas for recipes.

> "I always combine the wine with the sauce and not with the meat."
> Ingo Holland, Altes Gewürzamt, Klingenberg, Germany

"Red meat such as boiled beef may then, if it is not stewed, harmonize well with a strong white wine, such as Silvaner or even a barrel-aged Chardonnay. A sole on the bone, cooked with Vaucluse truffle-cream, screams, on the other hand, for a Pinot Noir."

Ingo Holland's cuisine cannot be pegged; he combines and processes products so that they go together in taste and smell. Whether they come from the same continent or not is a secondary concern: "I utilize spices where they are needed, where they accompany or complete something." He adheres to this philosophy with wine as well: "If you observe a few rules, it's not difficult to find the appropriate wine combination. You should taste the wine first, analyze its aromas, then put some thought into the dish and make the wine selection based on the corresponding flavors. Or the other way around. Apart from that, I would advise against extreme combinations–for example high acidity with sweet dishes, or light, fresh flavors with strong ingredients. In spite of all these considerations, I find it most exciting to first choose the wines you would like to pour in the course of an evening and to taste them, one after the other, to analyze their aromas and unique characteristics. From this information you can put together a wonderful menu that will then pair well with the wines. I find this method much more exciting than writing a menu and then choosing the wines for it. Especially with strongly seasoned or spicy hot dishes, it is important that highly acidic wines are avoided. I love to combine these dishes with reasonably mature and lightly sweet wines. So, for example, a mature Riesling from the Rheingau, where the acidity has already faded into the background and the sweetness builds a wonderful bridge to the strong flavors. I believe the combination of red wine and spicy curry, or the like, is problematic. On the other hand, robust grape varieties such as Cabernet Franc, Cabernet Sauvignon, Grenache, Syrah, etc. can by all means tolerate very strong spice flavors for example, pepper, bay leaves, juniper berries, and even chili."

The same holds true for **Dirk Niepoort**, an innovative traditionalist and culinary cosmopolitan. He travels the world on behalf of his wine and, on the way, he gets to know not only interesting people and good wines, but also a variety of culinary trends. "Basically, it is important to me that wines go with food, but I always think about the wine first. Then I try to adjust the different foods to match the wine. And by the way, I've never followed a recipe. I make my decisions dependent upon what comes to my mind, when I stroll across a farmer's market and see the fresh foods on offer. My cooking is based on local, natural ingredients. At home, I begin by choosing the wine, and only after that, I cook to match the wine. And in some cases depending on the mood my guests are in and which wines we open and when.

> "I begin by choosing the wine, and only after that, I cook to match the wine."
> Dirk Niepoort, Niepoort, Douro, Portugal

The result is then a more casual dinner spanning several courses. Sometimes I decide on the order of the courses, and above all what I want to cook, when everyone is already seated."

Riesling winemaker **Eva Clüsserath** from Trittenheim also cooks more spontaneously, but always fresh: "I usually start without a plan and use the ingredients that are available. Day-to-day I cook more local dishes, and I rarely follow recipes. Unfortunately, shopping has its challenges where we live, in the country. If I want something really special, it requires more planning and advance shopping."

Though Clüsserath doesn't always cook according to a recipe, she does have very specific dishes in mind which go with fruity Rieslings, rich in finesse: "Asian-style dishes harmonize perfectly with sweet Riesling, which have a delicate balance between juicy fruit, lively acidity, and a delicious sweetness." Following this, an excellent combination for a fruity Kabinett, in her eyes, is a spicy-hot curry-coconut soup: "Our Rieslings tend to go very well with fish, poultry, vegetables and light, not too powerful, sauces. A real insiders' tip is the combination of braised venison with mature (at least 15 years old) Riesling."

> "Have you ever tried a mature sweet
> Riesling Auslese with a braised leg of venison?
> It goes wonderfully together!"
> Eva Clüsserath, Weingut Ansgar Clüsserath, Mosel, Germany

When asked which wines are best suited to his cuisine, **Harald Rüssel** answered without hesitation: "Structured Rieslings, not bone-dry or even harsh, but "Mosel dry," hence in perfect balance between fruit, acidity and sweetness. If you try the wines with food, there must be a flavor kick in a positive way. Mature Mosel Riesling is an especially good match because it adapts splendidly to our strong-flavored authentic cuisine, while still keeping its character. The vintages 1971, 1975 and 1976 are currently showing perfectly, because fruit sweetness and acidity are deliciously integrated in its pleasant maturity. We cook exclusively with fresh, regional produce and "long-forgotten" foods. Through personal contact with local producers, I'm able to express personal wishes, and thus can significantly influence the quality."

"In the last few years I've done what a cook should spend a good
                portion of his time on: I looked for excellent local produce!"
Harald Rüssel, Landhaus St. Urban, Naurath, Germany (one Michelin star)

For **André Siebertz,** a native of the Rhine area, wine was a pleasant accompaniment to a meal until he met Christina Fischer. "I first had to learn how to differentiate a wine's taste, just like a dish. As a chef, one concentrates far too much on the ingredients of foods, their aromas and flavors, spices and the reciprocal effects. Then, it can happen that the suitable wine match gets pushed into the background, or is even forgotten." André Siebertz is curious and likes to experiment, so he is happy to explore the subject of wine. "I love subtle flavors, and it gives me great pleasure to tinker with compatible wine alliances." Thus, he maintains regular communication with the sommelier and service crew. "These discussions yield valuable experience and elementary knowledge for both sides, so we can take the next combination one step further." One of his defining moments was the effect of bitter-tasting rocket on a fruity, dry white wine. "The combination with the wine did not work, the bitter components gave the wine's fruitiness no chance. After we had exchanged the rocket with leeks, the wine was perfect!"

"If you want to work out a winning combination,
the wine must be, just like a dish, differentiated by its taste.
You can identify possible similarities or unharmonious,
contradictory elements in time, and counteract appropriately."

André Siebertz, Schloss Morsbroich, Leverkusen, Germany

Also, **Michael Kammermeier**, the chef at the "Ente" in Wiesbaden, is in constant communication with his sommelier in order to perfect his wine knowledge. Conversely, the sommelier benefits from Kammermeier's cooking knowledge. "This exchange helps me a lot, and at the same time gives me numerous ideas for new recipes, "Kammermeier says." If you understand that a wine is composed like a complex dish, the combination possibilities are endless. Because I love cooking with different sauces and fruits, like delicate aromas and new discoveries, the seemingly contradictory combinations are, for me, the real challenge. However, one must have an understanding of the basic rules in order to chance the tightrope walk of contradicting elements. One can quickly miss the mark, and then a total taste failure is imminent. The greatest thing is to create a major taste impact with just a few accents which are normally not considered to go with wine, but which ultimately provide the wine with the right link to be able to accompany the dish perfectly. "Whereby the emphasis is on the word 'accompany'!"

"In my view, wine and food should complement each other
and whet the appetite for the next bite or sip."

Michael Kammermeier, die Ente im Nassauer Hof,
Wiesbaden, Germany (one Michelin star)

When **Monika Fürst** wants to cook for a larger group, she has an extensive repertoire of suitable wine-friendly recipes. Her recommendation is: "Do the mental work well in advance. Appropriate menu consultation regarding the wines that will be tasted. Not too much variety on the plate, but preferably clear-cut structures. Good poultry, meat or fish solely from suppliers that we know. Ideally Bentheim pork and veal from France, tasty home-grown or organic vegetables (but only one!), high-quality cheeses and–no matter what–a pre-prepared dessert." When cooking and choosing the accompanying wines, Monika Fürst proceeds unpretentiously, very simply and with good taste. She prefers classic grape varieties. "In the summer, more light and fruity with a Silvaner or Riesling, in the winter it can be more intense and chocolaty, with a Frühburgunder or Pinot Noir."

"Very important is the type of preparation and the accompanying sauce. If it turns out more creamy and lemony-fresh, I like to combine a Pinot Blanc, while I prefer a Pinot Noir from Klingenberg with the rather strong flavors of stewed dishes."
Monika Fürst, Weingut Rudolf Fürst, Bürgstadt, Franken, Germany

Besides his family and his Palatinate winery, **Karl-Heinz Wehrheim** is passionate about many other things. He is an avid hunter, fishes for trout from his own pond and takes great delight in cooking. As to his opinion on whether or not a wine must be perfectly matched? "It should. Though I tend to experiment more and more. In the original Palatinate cuisine, plenty of thyme, marjoram and garlic are used. Today, in addition to these traditional herbs, Asian spices, ginger, coriander, lemongrass, wasabi and much more can be found. The cuisine has changed. Because of these intense and sometimes hot spices, the requirements for the accompanying wines have changed." Individuality is important to Karl-Heinz Wehrheim, not only in the wines but also in the cooking."It is very difficult for me to fight it, and therefore it is next to impossible for me to follow a recipe to the letter. If I have the framework for a recipe in my head, I improvise, completing it to my own taste and my momentary mood with different ingredients and spices. So it's possible that sometimes a mildly sweet sauce accompanies the venison or that the fish tastes of ginger! Because of this unorthodox style I need to taste and re-taste the food during cooking, and then be relatively flexible in choosing the right wine. I like to use Riesling and Pinot Blanc, perhaps because I like to drink them the most. Lighter styles can by all means be served at the beginning of a meal. Further along in the meal, of course, somewhat more compact and richer styles. Older, mature wines are always more exciting, in my opinion. Oak doesn't make any difference to me anymore, due to wisdom of (old) age, perhaps. I've brought wines back with me from every trip, so that is why–and this is important–it doesn't always have to be my own wine. So keep your eyes and ears open! My cooking style was clearly influenced by my mother. Back then, in the Wehrheim house on my grandmother's side, it was customary to cook Palatine-Alsatian cuisine. My mother, a native of Swabia, brought spaetzle and dumpling recipes from her homeland. An exciting combination!"

"Most importantly, recipes were rarely followed when cooking, but rather improvised freely–and the same was true for the seasonings. I copied this cooking style, and that is why I sometimes have to search a little longer for a matching wine."

Karl-Heinz Wehrheim, Weingut Dr. Wehrheim, Birkweiler, Pfalz, Germany

Whether a wine goes with the food is a pivotal question for the Franconian vintner **Hans Ruck**."Like in a good interpersonal relationship, the connection between wine and food should be characterized by harmony. One should not domineer over the other, but they should be mutually enhancing–and with this I always think of my Birgit!" If you ask Hans Ruck about

his cooking philosophy, he replies: "I like to cook regionally, with ingredients that the seasons have to offer in our Franconian homeland. Of course as a hunter, I can choose from an entire range of game, and lately I prefer deer and rabbit. We also have wonderful lamb and kid–a unique Franconian specialty. Whereby, of course, it very much comes down to the distinct natural aromas. Currently I devote my attention to low-temperature cooking. This is exactly the method that was used in the old days, without high-tech ovens and steam pressure-cookers, with fantastic results. Who has not dreamed of Grandma's Sunday roast, for which she got up at six in the morning, in time to shove it into the oven–which in this era most certainly didn't reach a temperature of 220 ° C. As with wine, good things take time. When selecting a wine, before anything else, the 'gradation' has to be right." For fresh, light dishes, such as appetizers and entrees, one chooses young, fresh wines. With increased flavor intensity in the menu sequence, a correspondingly more powerful wine must be chosen.

"Spices, depending on their intensity, require very compact and full-bodied wines, also because spicy heat generally comes into play, and in this situation, a simple, fruity wine is of no use."

Hans Ruck, Weingut Ruck, Iphofen, Franken, Germany

When **Frank Buchholz** isn't dealing with local products, he swears by Curry Wurst (Sausage in Curry-Ketchup Sauce) from "Pommes Heini" in Waltrop, with which he clearly prefers to drink a fresh, draft beer. "All in good time," is his motto, which he's followed for many years and true to this credo, he pairs Mediterranean–inspired cuisine with the wines of Rheinhessen. "I live in the country, and therefore like to use local products in my restaurant. Rheinhessen has refocused on its past, and has seen the evolution of a truly exciting food and wine culture, which connects agriculture and gastronomy in a traditional sense. I cook solely with fresh ingredients–for example, I very much like to use fresh herbs and spices, which I get from a neighboring gardener. I would basically describe my cuisine as light and fresh, which suits me very well on the wine side, because I love Riesling and Burgundian varieties."

"I make sure that the sauce goes with the wine and not the wine with the sauce."

Frank Buchholz, Buchholz Restaurant & Kochschule, Mainz, Germany (one Michelin star)

Ralf Bos loves and lives for food. He chooses the products for his delicatessen business with the eyes of an ambitious chef or sommelier. Bos considers it important that people re-introduce a little more food culture into their lives– particularly in Germany, where a cheap-and-cheerful mentality prevails with respect to grocery shopping. "People should enjoy more time in the kitchen with fresh ingredients, lots of fun and a spark of creativity! It's all about sharing the culinary pleasures of life in the company of family and friends." Most certainly with a glass of wine? "Of course!" grins Bos. "I even think it's important for the wines to go well with the meal. With the exception that when I feel like having a Sauvignon Blanc, I also drink it with ragout of wild boar, and when I feel like drinking a mature red Bordeaux, I sometimes even

enjoy a glass with steamed turbot. But in spite of all of this expertise, the focus should be on personal enjoyment. Apart from that, when pairing wine and food I focus mainly on the sauces and primary spices. This works well for food I'm familiar with, but when I'm confronted with unfamiliar dishes, I like to discuss the wine options with the sommelier". Bos eats out frequently, and when he does, he likes to try more elaborately prepared, extravagant dishes. At home, however, his cuisine is more Mediterranean, which put the product in the spotlight. "When I eat certain foods too frequently, their appeal diminishes after a while. There is one exception: truffles. At home during truffle season, we make eggs with truffles for breakfast. But my favorite dish is a Witzigmann classic: creamed spinach with fried eggs and shaved white truffles. With every product I ask myself the most important question of all: Can I improve its enjoyment in the glass or on the plate, and is the result at all feasible on a daily basis? Therefore, I advise my clients to consider these factors carefully. Those who follow this simple principle can look forward to satisfied guests and a resultant popularity over the long term."

"With every product I ask myself the most important question of all:
   Can I improve its enjoyment in the glass or on the plate, and
is the result at all feasible on a daily basis?"
Ralf Bos, bos food, Meerbusch, Germany

"Pastoral" is the name of his restaurant. Before **Bart de Pooter** and his wife moved there in 1991, this stalwart stone house was home to a rather simple bistro, and before that to the Pastor of Reet. Today, gourmets can enjoy delicious two-Michelin-star cuisine in a charming, unconventional atmosphere. Old wooden stairs, modern art, sleek white tablecloths, and cool black walls decorated with intertwining wooden slats seem to twist carelessly around the room. This bizarrely assembled creation from the artist Arne Quinze is synonymous with Bart de Pooter's vibrant gastronomy, reflecting its continuous evolution, and creating an all-around tasteful experience which is not only exceedingly pleasurable to the senses, but also heartwarming. Sommelier Jon Stalmans has been his boss's right-hand man for 16 years. "He is proud of the well-stocked wine cellar which houses, among other things, a respectable Riesling collection." De Pooter is one of those chefs who can cook to match a wine perfectly–in particular, Riesling. For others a real challenge, this varietal is, for him, one of the easiest to combine with food:

"A well-matured Riesling is characterized
        by perfectly balanced fruit sweetness
and acidity. This interplay results
in a multi-layered and expressive complexity–
    characteristics which I'm also looking
        for in my cuisine."
Bart de Pooter, Restaurant de Pastorale**,
        Reet, Belgium (two Michelin stars)

In addition to quality ingredients, de Pooter relies on different types of salt, using them purposefully: "We season more than we salt. But salt has an intensifying effect; it ensures a longer-lasting taste in the mouth." Bart de Pooter's cuisine is very clearly and puristically oriented. The quality of the food is the absolute focus. He plays with incisive acidity, delicate bitterness, tingling salt, and different textures in his cooking: "With which techniques can I convey the food's flavor as carefully as possible? Perhaps even lifting it to a higher level of taste quality?"

Lea Linster is convinced that chefs should not only serve haute cuisine: "A good chicken is like a good friend: it can never fail you!" To philosophize with her about the combination of wine and food is a great pleasure. Not just the recipes are close to her heart, but also the wine. After all, she is the proud owner of an Elbling vineyard on the Luxembourg Moselle river. She knows exactly what she's talking about. In an entertaining and mischievous fashion, she recounts her experiences with successful combinations. "The

right wine affords the palate a second glance. Have you ever tried caviar with a sweet Riesling? Much better than Champagne with caviar! This combination sounds more like brothel, casino, luxury and excess. Both have characteristics which are much too unique to be able to enter into a successful liaison, whereas with a mature late harvest wine, delicate aromas of fruit sweetness are set free which make the exciting, slightly salty taste of caviar seem much more intense."

"A bad combination between wine and food is an experience similar to brushing your teeth and then trying to drink Champagne."

Lea Linster, Cuisinière, Frisange, Luxembourg (one Michelin star)

When asked what his idea of the perfect culinary pleasure is, **Vincent Klink** started: "To feel pleasure, I must first be in good health. If wine and food can still be enjoyed, then it's bliss. Though for me, real bliss is having things only almost perfect. Complete perfection is too cold, almost inhuman." With this statement, he brings the search for perfection back down to earth. Whether it is important to him that the wine goes with the food? "If it does, I am happy, if it does not quite work, and the food is good, then I quietly tuck the bottle away in order to have more success with the second bottle. We have two sommeliers in house, and these gentlemen really throw themselves into the subject matter of wine purchasing and tasting. They have laid the proper groundwork, and because of this I feel very lucky. This has helped pave the way for my status as 'patron,' which is a really great job. For this reason I plan to manage the Wielandshöhe until I'm at least 80. Apart from that, I cook with my wonderful team by hook or by crook and the sommelier has to manage on his own. That is ultimately his job." Klink is an epicurean, and well aware of the basics of a successful combination: "I personally love complex wines—and when they can still hold their own against an oxtail dish despite having 12.5 percent alcohol, then these are the wines that go great with my cuisine. Nevertheless, some room must be made for whims. In life, it's a matter of supplying a daily illusion. Two decades ago, wines were so barrique-heavy that the Alsatian winegrower Jean Huegel was driven to exclaim, was the maker of this wine trained as a carpenter? Funnily, at that time most gourmets highly prized this oaky brew, and the reason for this is that often we don't react logically to certain fashions, including those which are utter nonsense. Therefore, one could say on a philosophical level that, no matter what, everything suits.

One man's meat is another man's poison, Huegel says. Sure there are criteria that are measurable, and nowadays there are food and wine reviews which are based on a scientific approach. There remain, however, the pitfalls of subjectivity and the danger that tongue and palate do not always function reliably. I recall some winemakers who didn't recognize their own product. With our cuisine I don't see great difficulties when pairing it with wine, since we cook very naturally. I expect the same standards from a wine."

"Everything that is created with respect for nature goes well together. It is similar to painting; when art is reduced to natural dyes, it is never displeasingly garish. Clearly, the fruity acidity of a young Riesling goes with chocolate, just like gasoline with pickled herring."

Vincent Klink, Wielandshöhe, Stuttgart, Germany (one Michelin star)

The Basis:
A Theoretical
Discussion

Passion with a System

The Pleasurable Interaction Between Wine and Food

Wine is part of an enjoyable life—and it is definitely part of a good meal. It doesn't have to be complicated: it starts with an everyday slice of bread topped with ham or cheese, and culminates in a multi-course gourmet menu. The most common question is, which wine goes with which food?

In this day and age of daily TV cooking shows and well-stocked grocery stores, wine merchants are often questioned about perfect combinations. Even though you can expect him or her to answer your question as readily and with the same skill as a sommelier, it is safest and easiest if you can make your own competent and independent decision about which wine will best match your cuisine. It doesn't hurt to acquire the basic skills and knowledge of a sommelier. This book is therefore not a dogmatic school, nor a panacea, but rather a guide for self-experimentation. Get familiar with your own taste, step-by-step, and gain understanding, glass by glass and bite by bite, of a craft that deals with the delicate interaction of wine and food, and enables you to make a confident and promising selection from a wine rack.

The Art of Pairing

The simplest introduction to the art of pairing is provided by culturally grown or regionally typical (and therefore comprehensible) connections: seafood and Muscadet, asparagus and Sylvaner, Riesling and Alsatian choucroute, or foie gras and sweet wines. If you enjoy these flavor combinations and want to improve your skills, you should take this opportunity to train your senses. The basics of every successful combination: recognize the taste components of different wines, and at the same time learn to identify the individual components of foods.

The understanding that every wine changes in its connection with food is the most important prerequisite for making perfect combinations.

In addition to the knowledge that every wine changes when combined with food, comes the relevant skills and knowledge of the taster—and, of course, his personal preferences, too. The human senses are an indispensable tool for this. The tongue, with its ability to perceive the basic tastes—sweet, sour, salty and bitter—is a taster's basic equipment. A fifth basic taste was discovered in 1908 by a Japanese scientist; called "umami," it is a salt of glutamic acid, an amino acid which is incorporated into proteins and has an intensifying effect on existing flavors. The result is a pleasant mouth feel, which enriches our sensory perception of both taste and touch. Umami is present in tomato paste, seaweed, beans and aged parmesan, but it is mainly present in soy protein. In conjunction with salt, umami acts as a catalyst for an intensely savory, stimulating taste, reminiscent of meat. The synthetically made flavor-enhancer glutamate has similar properties as umami and is, unfortunately, used far too disproportionately in the food industry.

Each taste experience is a very complex process, which is not only attributed to the sense of taste, but also to the senses of smell and touch. In some cases, even hearing plays a role: just think of crisp, crackling potato chips. Even eyesight affects our sense of taste, by raising expectations. You know the saying "a feast for the eyes"?

"Mouth feel" originates on the palate. This sensation is, in addition to the five basic tastes (sweet, sour, salty, bitter, umami), influenced by other parameters: structures and textures (crunchy, hard, soft, watery, etc.); fat (coating); astringent (drying out); and by stimuli (spicy, hot, cold).

Taste is therefore not only on the tip of the tongue, but also in the air. Taste would be impossible without aroma; the aroma molecules volatilize and find their way through the nose. A good 80 percent of flavor impression is determined by a variety of aromas. Only once in cooperation with the sense of smell is the brain capable of detecting the subtle differences. Constant "sniff training" is therefore a basic requirement for everyone who deals with wine and good food.

The nose is the key to a vast library of aromas–it is just often untrained.

Apart from protein, wine and food have very similar components which can interact with each other (see page 88, "A Systematic Approach to Food"). Experience has shown that wines, depending on their type, respond quite differently to the basic tastes and accompanying parameters such as fat, astringency, temperature and texture. How severe the reaction ends up being depends largely on the particular type of wine. Sweet, light wines react differently than medium-bodied, dry wines, or barrique-aged wines with marked tannins and a higher alcohol content. Some components are well-attuned, while others clash.

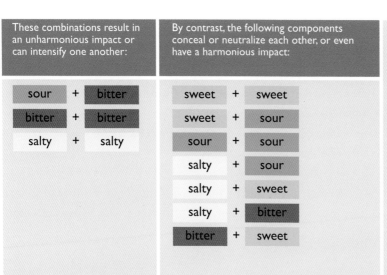

These combinations result in an unharmonious impact or can intensify one another:	By contrast, the following components conceal or neutralize each other, or even have a harmonious impact:
sour + bitter	sweet + sweet
bitter + bitter	sweet + sour
salty + salty	sour + sour
	salty + sour
	salty + sweet
	salty + bitter
	bitter + sweet

These rules are intended only for guidance. They serve as guidelines for general orientation and may be modified according to different concentrations and other influencing parameters.

For those who want to get more scientific, and want to research the subject of taste in more detail, we recommend the book "Kochuniversität Geschmack" by Thomas Vilgis.

Wine is Choosy

It is much more than the decision between fish or meat—the sauce, for instance, is a fundamental component which will bring excitement to the dish. Almost as important are the preparation and cooking methods: steamed, fried, grilled, roasted or even stewed? Which spices and herbs flavor the dish with what intensity, and how do other parameters determine or influence the overall impression of a dish?

Try to determine whether the wine and food components can complement each other or whether they create tension.

Most of us are familiar with these oft-repeated wine-and-food pairing rules, but must white wine only be served with white meat (fish and poultry) and red wine only with red meat (beef, lamb and game)? Frankly, if these rules ever had any validity, they are now long outdated. The basic set of rules for proper wine selection has evolved, and is now much more extensive. The main ingredient of a meal, i.e. fish or meat, is not the decisive component. Instead, try to define the influential taste elements of a dish, as well as those of the wine in question. Only those who recognize these will manage to achieve a deeper harmony between wine and food.

Bridge-building and Buffering

If all components of a dish are known, then wine can be integrated into the framework as a new component. Another important building block in this area is the knowledge of bridge-building and buffering options. Specifically, these include all kinds of vegetables and starchy foods such as potatoes, legumes, rice and pasta. Starchy foods can stretch or temper the effects of taste-intensive flavors, herbs, spices and sauces. A crispy potato-crusted fish fillet accompanied by sauerkraut and a cream sauce harmonizes well with a vibrant young Riesling. The trick: the starch in the potato crust buffers and tempers the acid in the sauerkraut as well as in the Riesling.

Vegetables generally have a neutral effect, but can be used in certain cases as a bridge to build a connection. Green beans, spinach or bell peppers can function as a transition to a red wine's tannins, but they can also be used as a catalyst. If tannins are in danger of disappearing behind the sweet-tasting flavor of a stew, a side dish of green beans or peppers can serve as a flavor-enhancing bridge.

A wine changes relatively little, as long as its aromas are in balance with the food's ingredients, and no intense element dominates the flavor. One of the easiest ways is to confront food with an equal wine partner. Dishes which are fine and complex in flavor usually require high-quality, complex wines. Simple and rustic dishes are best matched with simple, basic wines. A grilled fillet of turbot with a flavorful beurre blanc requires a complex, elegant Chardonnay with focused citrus flavors and delicate oak notes, whereas a hearty ham sandwich is best partnered with a simple, fruity, slightly chilled red wine with light tannins.

These accounts are only the beginnings of a long-lasting passion. The key tools–including strategic guidance for the right wine selection–can be accessed, bit by delicious bit, on the following pages. It is here, as elsewhere in life, that rules are sometimes made to be broken. Taste, smell and other senses are always just a snapshot, and this fleeting impression is different for every person.

It's the Sauce that Matters
The True Soul of a Dish

The traditional rule stating that white wine may be served with white meat (like fish and poultry), and red wine with red meat (such as beef, lamb and game), is history. This outdated principle totally ignores the individual characteristics of a dish, such as cooking methods, spices and, most notably, the sauces.

For a successful wine and food combination, the formative taste components of a dish are the primary focus. These include–in addition to intense herbs and spices that give the dish another taste dimension–the various cooking and preparation methods. The latter affects the taste of every roast, steak, fish, vegetable and side dish.

The sauce is the center of each dish,
because it combines the tastes of each individual flavor component.

What role does the sauce play in all of this? It is consumed with each bite, and hence affects all other components. The sauce is the undisputed center of every recipe.

Consider roast filet of beef, for example. The traditional rule states that red wine is the best match. That is true—only as long as the filet is served with, for example, a red wine shallot-jus. This same theory is false as soon as fried porcini mushrooms in a cream sauce accompany the meat. Of course, the roast beef has delicious, full-bodied aromas which could cozy up to the tannins of a powerful red wine, but a barrique-aged Chardonnay would be just as appropriate, especially when porcini mushrooms and cream come into play. On the contrary, the bitter tannins of an expansive red wine would have great difficulty coping with the abundance of creamy milk protein, and would respond with harsh astringency. The barrique-aged Chardonnay, on the other hand, bathes in the creamy sauce while its delicate creaminess and rich, fruit flavors are emphasized.

Increasing globalization is one reason why classic wine and food pairing rules are becoming obsolete. With the vast choices of ingredients, wines and cuisine styles, the range of possible combinations has expanded immeasurably. Classic, absolutely sure-fire combinations–such as turbot fillet in a creamy beurre blanc with elegant Meursault, or braised beef bourguignon with aged Gevrey-Chambertin–which were long-promoted by wine-friendly, gourmet cuisine–can now only rarely be found. Menus today offer more of a cross-cultural mix: Asian next to Oriental influences; Mediterranean-inspired recipes; French classical; molecular components; and regional ingredients.

So instead of just focusing on one main ingredient–such as beef, fish or poultry, whose preparation was determined as a matter of course in classic haute cuisine–other elements now come to the fore. With today's confusing variety of cooking methods, ingredients and cooking styles, it makes more sense to focus on the central, dominant flavor components of a dish. And, usually, it is well-advised to first focus on the sauce, and find its taste characteristics.

Why Are Sauces So Important?

To evaluate a good dish, there are at least as many criteria as are needed for the taste evaluation of a good wine. The same attention which is devoted to wine, to analyze its flavors and components, should be given to the dish with which the wine will be served. Since, as a rule, sauce dominates the taste impression of a meal, its preparation method is particularly crucial for choosing the perfect wine: What is the acidity of the sauce? How much of an influence does fat have on its taste? How intensely are roasted flavors perceived? Is it strongly reduced, influenced by certain spices, or very hot?

> As with wine, one should also determine
> the flavor components in food.

A good sauce has a life of its own; it is comparable to a small power plant. In addition to fat, it contains a good dose of acid (in the form of wine, lemon juice and vinegar) and salt, which gives the sauce a multi-layered complexity with a corresponding brilliance, similar to a high-quality wine. Without acid and salt, a sauce appears soft and lifeless. The fat, whether in the form of oil, cream, butter or lard, serves as the sauce's flavor carrier. Hence it is equivalent to the alcohol content of wine, which is also an important flavor carrier. Some sauces also have a good dose of sweetness. Packaged products hardly get by without this quite simple effect. As is the case with wine, sweetness categorically wraps itself around the tongue. Often this is just a cheap ploy to distract the consumer from any deficiencies.

In cuisine, a distinction is made between cold sauces; creamy, buttery sauces; and rich, dark sauces. These are called basic sauces.

Basic cold sauce	Basic white sauce	Basic brown sauce	Other basic sauces	Spicy sauces (preserved)
Vinaigrette Mayonnaise	Beurre Blanc (with fish stock) Velouté (with veal stock) Hollandaise Béchamel sauce	Poultry jus Veal jus Lamb jus Game jus	Tomato sauce	Chutney Chili sauce

Stock

A "stock" is nothing more than an unfinished sauce. It is a boiled-down broth, which is used for the completion of basic sauces. A tasty reduction of fish, shellfish, poultry, meat, lamb or game doesn't just taste like umami (see page 34), but is also the base for jus, gravy and other concentrated sauces.

Vinaigrette

A "vinaigrette" contains vinegar and, in most cases, also sugar. This presents most wines with an almost unsolvable problem. Tartaric acid and acetic acid do not get along particularly well. In order for wine to be able to hold its own next to vinaigrette, the vinaigrette should contain not only good quality oil, but also mild vinegar and fresh broth. Mustard is excellent for binding; because of its acidity, however, it should be used very carefully.

Basic White Sauce

White sauces are refined with cream, usually bound with butter, and have a smooth, creamy texture. Beurre blanc is one of the most important white sauces in fine cuisine. With its delicate, buttery, fine lemony flavor, it can be modified in many different ways. Numerous versions–such as with fresh herbs, mustard or balsamic vinegar–can be made.

Jus

A dark jus, or gravy, is made by roasting bones and adding roasted vegetables, red wine and tomato paste. The entire mass is repeatedly doused with liquid, usually a stock, and seared until it is, once again, reduced. Finally, the sauce is passed through a cloth, and again reduced until a maximum of one third of the original volume remains. The result is a strong base sauce with integrated, roasted aromas and a fine acid structure that comes from the red wine and tomato paste. Jus is very versatile; a variety of sauces can be conjured from it, such as rosemary jus, port-wine sauce or red wine-shallot sauce.

Interaction Between Wine and Sauce

Each sauce has individual, defined taste elements that must be kept in mind when combined with wine. When these elements are known, a sauce–and often an entire dish–can be modified to match the characteristics of a particular wine. This requires the knowledge of their components and how they interact with one another. They are:

- Acidity
- Sweetness
- Caramel
- Creaminess (comes from the fat portion)
- Bitterness
- Saltiness

A more concentrated sauce can be achieved by further reduction. The finished sauces and their variations can get a flavor boost from the following spices and aromatic compounds:

- Chili (hot spice)
- Salt content (marinades)
- Umami (soy sauce)
- Special spices and herbs
- Aromas (volatile)

The Thrilling Contrast of Flavors
Nature's Modular System

Smell and taste are individual sensations and, as such, are subjective. Both have the same chemical compounds as a base. Whether they are found in fruit, vegetables or wine, these compounds are often identical or even related, and thus the foundation of our flavor library.

Scents and Smells

Nature is equipped with an extensive repertoire of chemical compounds which are responsible for odors and scents. Nature utilizes time-proven compounds over and over. They are found in fruits and vegetables, just as in wine.

Modern science currently refers to more than a thousand different scents and flavors. When one eats or drinks something, the respective sensory organs transport flavors into the mouth and nose. The impact of the sense of smell should not be underestimated. This sensory perception takes place in the back of the palate, where there is a direct connection to the brain's olfactory center. From there comes the message, for example, that something tastes like lemon or lime. This sensitive distinction is not made in the mouth, but in the olfactory center of the brain–in its well-stocked aroma library. There, the aromas are reviewed, and then sorted and classified at full speed.

Someone who works intensively with food, wine, and their combinations will, over time, develop a vast orientational knowledge of flavors. Storing his or her acquired impressions, he or she is capable of quickly retrieving them at a later time. This is a question of conscious and trained perception and recognition. The more odors and scents are actively stored, the better, faster and more precisely the task of aroma recognition, recall and identification can be accomplished.

In the aroma library of our brain, the different aromas and flavors are sorted and classified at full speed.

During a meal, numerous taste sensations intertwine which, on the whole and in their interaction, leave a totally different impression. The pitfall lies in the fact that in a traditional dish, (meat or fish, sauce, spices, herbs, vegetables and side dishes) different components are discerned. Depending on the order in which the individual components reach the palate and nose, their impact on the accompanying wine will vary. Added to that is the reciprocal interaction of wine and food. A wine usually tastes completely different on its own than in the company of food. As a matter of fact, there are wines that only develop their true flavor with the appropriate dish.

Now, where should you begin? Which parameters are fundamentally important? In this case, practice makes perfect. It is much easier to recognize a harmonious combination between wine and food than it is to create a successful, at first seemingly contradictory, connection between wine and food, which provides stimulating tension and enhanced enjoyment. For this you need some practice, and a keen interest in wine as well as food and its different preparation methods.

The ideal situation for every beginner would be if the wine and food combination were to form a perfectly harmonious taste. Unfortunately, this is a rare occurence. A normal dish consists of various components and the wine must be harmonious with all its ingredients. Since the wine can't be altered, you should use your existing knowledge and modify the non-compatible ingredients a bit to suit the wine. The successful outcome does not cost a lot of effort, but allows both the wine and the food the necessary freedom to let their individual tastes unfold.

Furthermore, a dish can be offset with contradicting or opposite flavors. Think of a fat goose, which literally perks up in the company of a fruity, fresh, slightly acidic Pinot Noir. If you paired this dish with a strong, slightly jammy, alcoholic Australian Shiraz, you would likely choke on this fatty morsel. The Pinot Noir has an almost catalyzing effect; it supports the dish, lifts the flavors, and lends the necessary balance to the palate with its fresh acidity.

Kindred by Choice

The Regional Link Between Wine and Food

Historically, wines of a specific region were traditionally consumed with their own region's customary cuisine. That is why these wines go well with tradition-rich regional recipes, such as seafood with Muscadet; boeuf bourguignon with Pinot Noir; venison and truffles with Barolo; choucroute with Alsatian Riesling; and asparagus with Silvaner.

The Culturally Evolved Relationship Between Wine and Food

Culturally evolved, time-proven combinations–like foie gras and noble sweet wines, or Stilton and Port–captivate time and time again.

The Harmonious Relationship of Flavors

If you know the flavors of wine and food, it's easy to create a harmonious connection. Once the flavors in wine and food are balanced, the wine will barely change. When related flavors meet, like green beans and the grassy notes of a Sauvignon Blanc, flavor harmony is achieved. The grape variety Cabernet Sauvignon, with its aromas of green bell pepper, is well-suited to dishes with bell peppers, while a buttery, barrel-aged Chardonnay snuggles up perfectly with rich, cream-based sauces. With a little practice in this area, one can quickly reach success.

Harmony by Contrasting Flavors

With this type of combination you need, in addition to extensive product knowledge, a sure instinct and a wealth of experience. Complementary or even contrasting flavors of wine and food can trigger that final flavor kick. A fat roast goose, for example, is well-matched with an elegant, fruity Pinot Noir, but for more reasons than just harmony: the wine boosts its flavors and the goose can shine in the spotlight. Older, mature, somewhat-tired wines can benefit when they are served with fish and meat dishes in combination with a salad. The vinaigrette's acidity gives the mature wine some much-needed freshness. Multi-faceted dishes with many taste components and aromas can push simple wines into the spotlight. These wines can be much more straightforward, simple and accommodating to the self-centered dish than an attention-loving complex wine could be. The simpler wine will show its thanks with exciting and fruity liveliness. With this combination method, however, one walks a fine line. Even the slightest misstep can cause the taste to take a tailspin.

The Taste Relationship Between Wine and Food

First, one must be aware of the main characteristics of both the wine and food in question. What is the relationship between sweetness, acidity, salt-content, alcohol, fat content, spice, tannins and bitterness? Harmony is created as soon as these characteristics meet their wine or food counterpart. To be sure, this requires a solid, basic knowledge of the various ingredients, wine components and their possible combinations. Sophisticated dishes require complex, multi-layered wines, while a regional, country-style dish calls for a more quaffable, basic wine. This is the kind of knowledge which helps to create a wine-and-food pairing experience with that extra something–and explains why you need several years of regular training to be able to create successful combinations.

A Systematic
Approach to Wine

Why Wine Types?

The Necessary Tools for Successful Combinations

When selecting wine, most people generally distinguish wines by color: white, rosé or red. And when it comes to pairing wine with food, the oldest and most absurd of all clichés comes to the table: red wine with red meat, white wine with white meat and fish or poultry.

If you are satisfied with this rule, you should realize by now that it's time for to close this book. If you have a healthy curiosity and a corresponding thirst for knowledge, you are in exactly the right place. After covering aromas, flavors, guiding principles and basic rules in the first chapter, we now devote ourselves exclusively to the liquid side: wine. This chapter will highlight a sensible classification and categorization of the different types of wine in an easy-to-understand manner.

Food changes the taste of wine more often than the other way around. Wine is bottled as a finished product, and changes only through maturation. Foods, however, are governed by recipes which can be modified at any time. Therefore, it would make more sense to first choose the wine before deciding what to cook or optimizing the dishes to match the wine you want to drink. This, unfortunately, is a high aspiration which cannot realistically be put into practice in normal restaurant service.

Another finding has led me to create a fundamental division of the extensive selection of wine on offer today: wines, regardless of their colors, may respond in similar ways with food. The classification by color is, therefore, of limited use. Chill down a light, fruity red wine and taste it. When tasting blind, you will hardly be able to differentiate it from a white wine. And what about classifying according to the grape variety? Even this classification is not reasonable, because many wines are blends of several varieties. Moreover, very different wines can be made from the same grape variety–from simple jug wines all the way up to Grand Cru wines!

The American chef and Master Sommelier Jerry Comfort has devoted himself to wine and food pairing for almost 20 years. His discoveries hold delicious and, above all, exciting potential. He divides the vast wine world into categories. "It all depends on how a wine is made–which style it's made in and how it tastes–and not necessarily out of which grape variety it's made." (www.beringer.com/wine-food-pairing)

Such a classification makes sense, because a clear, universally comprehensible wine description is difficult to formulate. Most wine drinkers are insecure, and are much more capable of giving a description of their favorite type of wine than they are of giving exact information on vintage, wine producer and wine region. Therefore, a useful system–a classification of wine types–is perhaps a practical way to approach a seemingly complicated topic in a simple manner.

How does the classification by wine type work?

The next few pages will include a summary in table form, followed by the classifications and detailed descriptions of the different wine types. These categorizations will serve as a useful tool for the proceeding wine-culinary chapters. This categorization is not straightforward, and it is perhaps even over-ambitious. A wine expert who undertakes an in-depth examination of this system can certainly find weak points. Typical examples can be found to represent each category, but there are also counter-examples and exceptions. And there is always some overlap across categories. Of course, not all Bordeaux wines are complex and elegant, and not all New World wines are opulent, bold and high in alcohol. New World wines are perhaps already a step ahead, because today, elegance and complexity are very meticulously sought out, and therefore vineyards are planted in cooler regions and higher altitudes. A new, much more elegant style of wine is thus emerging!

Exceptions and special cases can never be ruled out in this model, but that's what makes wine so interesting. Nevertheless, the majority of wines can be covered in this categorization. You will refer to these wine types throughout the entire book. In every table they are depicted by stylized, colored wine glasses. They should assist you in your wine selection and, most of all, they should provide a certain reliability.

Search and find the right type ...

Wine Types	Wine Type 1 Light and Fresh	Wine Type 2 Fruity and Harmonious	Wine Type 3 Complex and Elegant	Wine Type 4 Powerful and Opulent
Description	fresh, fruity, lean, light wine, usually vinified in stainless steel (unoaked)	medium-bodied, pleasantly quaffable wine with delicate creamy texture and balanced fruit aromas, with or without oak notes	complex, multi-faceted wine with tension and elegance, has a good length and aging potential, perfectly integrated oak notes or vinified in stainless steel	powerful, concentrated wine with opulence, noticeable alcohol, stainless steel vinification or with distinct oak notes
Fruit	clear fruit aromas, derives its appeal from a lively lightness and, in southern regions, from youthful character	from fruity to ripe aromas, medium intensity, in some cases with spicy, herbal components	delicately fruity, clearly defined, complex aromas with brilliant structure and powerful finish	very intense, lusciously ripe and expressive aromas, juicy, heavy, in some cases overripe
Acidity	crisp, from fresh to lively, animating acidity	moderate, harmoniously integrated, mild to juicy acidity	perfectly integrated, lively acidity which lends backbone and structure	very ripe, low acidity, alcohol dominates
White Wines	Less than 12% Vol.	12-13.5% Vol.	12.5-13.5% Vol.	over 13.5% Vol.
	Kabinett, Germany Elbling Müller-Thurgau Gutedel Steinfeder, Wachau, Austria Styrian Junker, Austria Entre-Deux-Mers, Bordeaux Muscadet, Loire Vinho Verde, Portugal Pénedes white wines Hárslevelü, Hungary	Silvaner, Scheurebe Pinot Gris and Pinot Blanc Styrian Classic, Austria Federspiel, Wachau, Austria DAC white wines, Austria Fendant, Switzerland Touraine, Loire Chenin Blanc, Loire Italian white wines Verdejo, Rueda, Spain Furmint, Hungary Eastern European white wines New World white wines	Riesling Grosses Gewächs Cru Sauvignon Blanc, Styria, Austria Premier & Grand Cru Burgundy Premier & Grand Cru Chablis Sancerre & Pouilly Fumé, Loire Bordeaux Blanc, Graves Cru Sauvignon Blanc, Alto Adige Dézaley, Switzerland Chardonnay, cool climate	Ruländer/Pinot Gris Gewürztraminer Smaragd, Wachau, Austria Grand Cru, Alsace Vouvray, Loire Condrieu, Rhône Marsanne-Roussanne Vin Jaune, Jura Oaked Chardonnay, New and Old world
Red Wines	Less than 12.5% Vol.	12.5-14.0% Vol.	12.5-14.0% Vol.	over 14.0% Vol.
	Trollinger Beaujolais Côtes de Bourg Rosé Bardolino Vernatsch	Pinot Noir Dornfelder, Lemberger Zweigelt, St. Laurent DAC red wines, Austria Cabernet Franc, Loire Beaujolais Cru Bordeaux Côtes du Rhône Languedoc-Roussillon Valpolicella, Dolcetto Rosso di Montepulciano Tempranillo, basic Portuguese red wines Pinotage Red wines, international	Pinot Noir Cru Blaufränkisch Bordeaux Cru Côte-Rôtie Hermitage Roussillon Barbaresco Chianti Classico Riserva Brunello di Montalcino Barolo Rioja Ribera del Duero Premium New World Cabernet Sauvignon	Red wine cuvées, international Blaufränkisch Reserve Châteauneuf-du-Pape Amarone Toro Priorat Douro Dão Zinfandel Merlot Malbec Shiraz

Wine Types	Wine Type 1 Light and Fresh	Wine Type 2 Fruity and Harmonious	Wine Type 3 Complex and Elegant	Wine Type 4 Powerful and Opulent
Description	fresh, fruity, lean, light wine, usually vinified in stainless steel (unoaked)	medium-bodied, pleasantly quaffable wine with delicate, creamy texture and balanced fruit aromas, with or without oak notes	complex, multi-faceted wine with tension and elegance, has a good length and aging potential, perfectly integrated oak notes or vinified in stainless steel	powerful, concentrated wine with opulence, noticeable alcohol, stainless steel vinification or with distinct oak notes
Fruit	clear fruit aromas, derives its appeal from a lively lightness and in southern regions from youthful character	from fruity to ripe aromas, medium intensity, in some cases with spicy, herbal components	delicately fruity, clearly defined, complex aromas with brilliant structure and powerful finish	very intense, lusciously ripe and expressive aromas, juicy, heavy, in some cases overripe
Acidity	crisp, from fresh to lively, animating acidity	moderate, harmoniously integrated, mild to juicy acidity	perfectly integrated, lively acidity which lends backbone and structure	very ripe, low acidity, alcohol dominates
Sparkling Wines	Less than 12.5% Vol.	12.0-12.5% Vol.	12.0-12.5% Vol.	11.0-15.0% Vol.
	basic branded Sekt Frizzante Semi-sparkling wine	Grower's Sekt Champagne Crémant, Cava Spumante, Cap Classique Brazilian Sparkling	Vintage Champagne Special cuvées with delicate oak notes (Krug, Jacquesson, Bollinger)	Crimean sparkling Sparkling Shiraz
Sweet Wines	7.0-10.0% Vol.	7.5-13.0% Vol.	6.5-12.5% Vol.	12.5-16.0% Vol.
	Riesling Kabinett (Mosel, Rhein, Nahe) Moscato d'Asti (from 4.5% Vol.)	Spätlese Vendanges tardives Gewürztraminer Recioto di Soave Rosenmuskateller/Moscato Rosa Late Harvest "New World" New World Moscato	Auslese Beerenauslese (BA) Trockenbeerenauslese (TBA) Eiswein/Ice wine Ausbruch (Rust, Austria) Quarts de Chaume Coteaux du Layon Jurançon and Tokaji Aszú	Sélection de Grains Nobles Gewürztraminer (Edelsüß/noble sweet) Strohwein, Vin de paille (from dried grapes) Sauternes, Monbazillac Recioto della Valpolicella Vin Santo Moscato Passito di Pantelleria, Sicilly Constantia, South Africa
Fortified Wines		14.0-18.0% Vol.	15.0-20.0% Vol.	18.0-22.0% Vol.
		Dry: Manzanilla & Fino Sherry Madeira Sercial White Port, dry Sweet: Banyuls and Maury Muscat de Rivesaltes Muscat de Beaumes de Venise Ruby Tawny, young LBV Port	Dry: Amontillado Sherry Palo Cortado Madeira Verdelho Sweet: Banyuls Grand Cru Madeira Bual Tawny, 30 or 40 years old Colheita Port Vintage Port	Dry: Oloroso Sherry Sweet: Malmsey Madeira Marsala Pedro Ximenez Sherry Cream Sherry Montilla-Moriles Orange and Black Muscat, California Brown Muscat, Australia

White Wine Type I 🍷
Light and Fresh

Light wines should be refreshingly light, but not thin or watery to the taste. For this category, a low alcohol content is the most important requirement. The spectrum of this wine type is broad, from delicious, everyday easy-drinking wines and uncomplicated bag-in-box wines, to jug wines and finely crafted Kabinett wines. Expressive, light wines come primarily from northern growing areas. There, the weather is cooler compared to southern growing areas. This moderate climate provides a much longer growing season which allows the grapes to develop fresh fruit flavors without losing their refreshing acidity. Such Kabinett wines are—traditionally and as required by law—refreshingly light but with lots of flavor, and have 12 percent or less alcohol by volume. They come mainly from the northern growing areas such as Mosel, Saar, Ruwer, Mittelrhein, Nahe, Rheingau, Saale-Unstrut and Saxony.

In general, light wines are often culturally evolved, local specialties, mostly from indigenous varieties. A typical example is the traditional Elbling variety, which grows mainly on the Mosel River, both on the Luxembourg and German sides. Austrian white wines have some stimulating offerings in this category: light Grüner Veltliner Steinfeder from the Wachau; delicately spicy Welschriesling; or aromatic Muskateller from Styria. There are traditionally light, fresh wines that come from some of the warmer regions, which benefit from youthful, stimulating, yeasty notes and a refreshing lightness. Delicious examples are: invigorating Muscadets from the Loire; aromatic Entre-Deux-Mers from the Bordeaux region; or effervescent Portuguese Vinho Verde.

Whimsical wines,
    summer sippers or robust individualists.

Apart from classic Kabinett wines of the northern growing areas, these light-weights are usually vinified reductively (without oxygen) in stainless steel tanks at controlled temperatures. They excel mainly with crisp freshness as well as primary fruit aromas and flavors. While they pair well with some foods, they aren't necessarily perfect companions in a menu. But that's not their job; rather, they are whimsical, summer sipping wines or robust rebels, and they don't take offense if we do not give them our undivided attention.

What's more, they are ideal as an aperitif in place of a Kir, or fad cocktails such as the Spritz. Their carefree, fresh style whets the appetite for a delicious meal. It is advisable to buy the youngest possible vintages and to drink them as soon as possible, because their aging capacity is limited. An exception in this category is dry Riesling Kabinett which, even after three to five years of bottle age, will not have lost any of its freshness. It will also have developed an incredible aroma and flavor complexity.

White Wine Type 2 🍷🍷
Fruity and Harmonious

The most typical characteristic of these wines is to be harmonious, mainly because all of their components–extract, flavor, acidity, alcohol and fruit–are well-balanced. These are medium-bodied, dry wines with delicious fruit intensity. This classic type of white wine is produced all over the world, and with its moderate alcohol content of 12 to 13.5 percent by volume, it accounts for more than half of the international white wine production. Depending on region of origin and age, these middleweights display fresh to juicy ripe notes; pleasantly mild to juicy acidity; and, in some cases, even some spicy aroma components.

Everyday food companions with fruity creaminess
and balance.

Due to their moderate intensity, these wines can be vinified both with and without oak barrels. The options include concrete; plastic or stainless-steel tanks; wood chips; large wooden casks; or barriques. With this wine type, however, the wood which has been used in its vinification is, at best, only indirectly detectible as a supporting element. This category includes most single varietal wines–Pinot Gris, Pinot Blanc, Riesling, Sylvaner, some regional specialties such as Grüner Veltliner, Chenin Blanc, Verdejo, Torrontés–but also international varieties such as Sauvignon Blanc or Chardonnay.

This wine type is the force behind many successful wine concepts; for example, the Rheinhessen Selection or DC Pfalz, which profiles regionally typical grape varieties. Similarly, Austrians have created a wine type with a high recognition value: their Styrian Classic (Sauvignon Blanc, Morillon, Pinot Blanc). The Austrian DAC concept (Districtus Austriae Controllatus), in the same way, sets clear signals for the recognition of regionally typical, quality wines. Conforming to this distinctive profile are Grüner Veltliner wines from the Weinviertel, as well as from the regions Traisental, Kremstal and Kamptal, in which Riesling is also allowed. In addition, Northern Italy and especially South Tyrol offer a remarkable selection of delicious middleweights with spicy, savory aromas. The range is abundant: from Pinot Grigio and Pinot Blanc, to Chardonnay and Traminer. In fact, indigenous varieties play a dominant role in some countries; For example Rueda with Verdejo, Galicia with Albariño, Hungary with Furmint, Switzerland with Chasselas, or the Loire with Chenin Blanc.

In the New World, it was quickly understood that Chardonnay and other white wines need not always be oaky, big and flabby. In the meantime, white wines from the Southern Hemisphere were being made in temperature-controlled stainless steel tanks in order to preserve primary fruit flavors as well as the corresponding, stimulating freshness. This trend also illustrates the global success of Sauvignon Blanc. Thanks to careful vinification, the harmoniously lush, medium-bodied wines of this type can be easily produced almost everywhere. For most, they offer daily enjoyment with a fruity creaminess and a well-balanced character.

White Wine Type 3 ♉♉♉
Complex and Elegant

"Complexity" is a commonly used term for wines that are both multi-layered and full of finesse. When the attribute "elegant" is added to such a wine description, a profound wine with structure and character is being described. Among wine connoisseurs, this is certainly one of the most sought-after wine types of them all. They are the exact opposite of everyday wines.

Wine personalities which deserve extra attention.

Wine personalities which deserve extra attention can, perhaps, be compared to the complex creations made by starred chefs, which consist of many individual elements and taste facets. These wines are often closed and inexpressive in their youth, when they reveal only a small portion of their complexity. As youngsters, they dominate a wine tasting with their bold and fruit-forward style. But after a few years, they wake up from a deep sleep, polished and refined.

One of its main features is the fact that its finesse and complexity increases with bottle age. Prerequisites for this are a moderate climate, a long growing season, and moderate to low yields. The goal is to pick the grapes at their optimum physiological ripeness without allowing their sugar level to skyrocket which, during the subsequent fermentation, would result in an undesirably high alcohol level. The later the harvest date, the closer the grapes reach the point of full maturity, and the more pronounced and intense the flavor development. This lends this wine type an elegant taste.

Terroir—a complex term, which loosely means "a sense of place" and refers to the soil type, topography, grape variety, winemaking and climate—plays a crucial role. Thus you find these wines mainly in the temperate zones of Europe, and particularly in long-established quality wine regions. Even if a winery has the most modern technology, in the end the wine's quality is determined exclusively in the vineyard. The winemaker merely guides the wines through vinification, carefully making minute adjustments without major interventions. Thus, one often vinifies without wood, or uses it very cautiously. Large wooden casks (30-700 hl) provide a supportive backbone, while smaller-sized barriques impart structure as well as aromatic components. The German Riesling Grosses Gewächs (Grand Cru), usually spends no time in wood or, if it does, then only in large, or seasoned wine barrels. Every elegant Burgundian Chardonnay, however, is matured and almost always fermented in small, 225-liter barriques (called "pieces"). This is, by the way, the standard by which the rest of the wine world is oriented with respect to barrel use, complexity and elegance. These wines go well with food and have considerable aging potential. The well-integrated yet perceptible acidity creates tension and structure. This, in combination with complex flavors, extracts and balanced alcohol, provides a fluid counterpoint to many dishes.

White Wine Type 4
Powerful and Opulent

In the case of this wine type, the "devil is in the details." For within this category there are, again, different styles. Those wishing to explore the entire spectrum must surrender themselves to these wines' lush vibrations, and yield to the seductive alcohol which pleasantly numbs the palate. These generous wine types can taste lusciously fruity, juicy, creamy and expansive, but also spicy or toasty, and these potent combinations challenge the palate.

Powerhouses with a pleasantly lush stature.

Depending on the philosophy of the winemaker, this expansive wine type can be devoid of any perceptible wood flavors, such as the utterly creamy tasting Pinot Gris from the Alsace and Baden. And similary, gorgeously concentrated Wachau Grüner Veltliner Smaragd, spicy Alsatian Gewürztraminer, or quaffable and creamy Pinot Blanc from South Tyrol.

On the opposite end of the spectrum are wines with a deliberate, significantly perceptible oak-barrel influence. These powerhouses are usually of a more opulent stature. They deliver a punch, because their high alcohol content (more than 14 percent) place them in a precarious situation bordering on both pleasure and pain.

There is a danger that its taste can fall apart into a kind of boring rusticity. This can only effectively be counter-balanced with lush, ripe fruit notes; structure-giving extracts; or savory, phenolic compounds. This can be attained either by maceration–by which aroma and bitter compounds are extracted from the grape skins–or by the targeted use of new or used oak barrels. These winemaking techniques get full-bodied wines "into shape," so to speak, whereby the high alcohol is assimilated and perfectly masked by the wood. In the best case, the result is a balanced, full-bodied wine which, in addition to its luscious character, offers balanced flavors and aromas; a touch of invigorating acidity; and stimulating astringency.

This wine type is produced mainly in the warmer regions of Europe, and especially in the Southern Hemisphere, so it is always influenced by abundant sunshine.

The extreme temperatures ensure the grapes ripen very quickly, which causes the acidity to drop in exchange for increased sugar accumulation. As a result, the end-product wine has a high degree of ripeness, which can very well be linked to low acidity and possibly higher alcohol levels.

This wine type, modeled after Burgundian Chardonnays, emerged in the late 1990s, and is now found all over the world in various forms. In general, these wines are very concentrated, ripe powerhouses whose sweet impressions (which stem from oak as well as from alcohol content) are only just perceptible in the aftertaste. These concentrated and frequently full-bodied wines have a distinct character, and are, therefore, not easy to combine with food; they would most likely sweep a delicious ham sandwich off the table.

Their ripe, sweet-tasting opulence—which is supported by elevated alcohol levels—creates blockbuster wines. At the table, their power must be counter-balanced by acid, salt, savory spices, or even bitter-tasting roasted flavors. And don't forget to always incorporate a good dose of fat in the dish in the form of butter, creamy beurre blanc, or even foie gras. Then, they can even take on the role of the classical red-wine accompaniment—as a pairing with venison or meat dishes—without the slightest effort.

Red Wine Type I 🍷
Light and Fresh

Some call this a thin, wimpy, anemic red-hued wine, while others enjoy it precisely for its delightfully delicious lightness. This sympathetic, light wine type needs very little tannin, because its charm lies more in its youthful freshness and its fruity drinkability. In producing these uncomplicated wines, the must (pressed grapes and juice) stays in contact with the grape skins for only a short time. This keeps its color light, the bitter and astringent tannins very low, the fruit flavors fresh, and its character lively and approachable. Astringent tannins from the skins, seeds and stems are hardly found in these wines, if at all. The subsequent storage in steel tanks, or large, used casks serves the same purpose.

A red wine in conflict.

A characteristic freshness brings this wine type in very close kinship with many white wines and rosés. Some of the grape varieties used for this type cannot get much deeper in color than a dark rosé (e.g. Trollinger, Pinot Noir). A rosé of Cabernet Sauvignon, on the other hand, sometimes has a darker color than some of these light reds!

The grape varieties will have more or less of an impact on the taste of the finished wine, depending on the winemaking methods used. Rosé wines play an important role in this group. They can be produced in different ways: The dark grapes are pressed after a short maceration, which results in a rosé wine with a dinstinctly red color. Another common method is to press whole bunches that will produce a very pale must, which is usually bottled as Blanc de Noir. If, however, the goal is to make a slightly darker rosé, the "saignée method" is used to give the wine additional color. About 10 to 15 percent of the must from the red wine-fermentation tanks is removed, blended with the pale juice, and then vinified as a rosé wine. As a beneficial side effect of this process, the remaining red wine undergoes a natural concentration due to the higher ratio of skin to juice. Another rosé wine production-method is the blending of white and red wines.

Such a blend is not permitted to be labeled as a rosé, but as Rotling. Schiller Wine, Badisch Rotgold and Saxony Schieler are all examples of Rotlings. Another wine style in this category of light reds is the now-almost-forgotten Claret, which has a slightly deeper color compared to most rosés. In the Middle Ages, Claret was synonymous with Bordeaux wines, and was exported in large quantities to England. This wine is only briefly fermented with the skins, so as not to re-lease too much color and tan-nin into the wine.

Apart from all of these different rosé wines are red wines that have undergone a traditional red wine-vinification, yet still belong in this category of drinkable lightweights: Trollinger, Portugieser, South Tyrolean Vernatsch, and simple Beaujolais wine are all examples of this wine type. Bardolino and straightforward Valpolicella, as well as classically vinified Bordeaux wines from Côtes de Blaye and Côtes de Bourg, also fit this definition. All of these uncomplicated red wines should be served chilled, at a temperature of 15 degrees Celsius (rosé between 7-10 degrees Celsius). Chilling this light-red wine type is not a crime; rather, it is useful to improve its drinking pleasure. These wines pair well with cheese, charcuterie and bread in an uncompli-cated daily wine-culture.

Red Wine Type 2 🍷🍷
Fruity and Harmonious

This category includes all the regionally typical classics, as well as international, harmonious red wines. These are medium-bodied, aromatic, juicy red wines with well-integrated tannins, a moderate alcohol level and a pleasant length. They're found in every wine cellar, and they're also daily food companions that fulfill a higher standard and have a good palate weight. In addition, these unpretentious all-rounders are universally compatible; they are capable of dealing with all sorts of occasions quite easily. Modern winemaking is largely responsible for this. Winemakers have ways to pleasantly emphasize the fruit aromas and to support the wines very simply with a velvety, well-integrated tannin structure. The result is pleasantly harmonious, the kind of drinking pleasure you don't have to think too long and hard about. Challenges to the palate, such as unpleasantly rough astringency; high acidity; overpowering alcohol; or dominating toasty oak flavors are rather rare in this wine type.

> Universally compatible,
> unpretentious all-rounder.

This type of medium-bodied red wine is found mainly in the south of Germany, while it is generally found in all areas of the Mediterranean. This wine type is even prevalent in Switzerland, and we can also expect more to come from Eastern Europe in the next few years. With the term DAC (Districtus Austriae Controllatus), Austria has created an additional geographical designation, parallel to its existing system for quality wines. For example, wines made from the Blaufränkisch variety are exemplary for the Mittelburgenland region and those wines which have the Mittelburgenland DAC designation demonstrate a typical regional and flavor profile. This system is very advantageous as the wines are clearly recognizable for the consumer. This kind of varietal tipicity is also found in Pinot Noir from regions such as Ahr, Pfalz and Baden, wines from Rioja, Côte du Rhône and even in simple Burgundy wines. In South Africa, Australia, Chile, Argentina, California and the rest of the world, these are less regionally typical wines than the pure varietal or brand names that describe the medium-bodied wine type. Overall, it is a very good

starting point for novice wine drinkers. Apart from a few original varieties, such as South African Pinotage and Chilean Carménère, red wines from the New World are mostly blends of the classic Bordeaux varieties Cabernet Sauvignon and Merlot. Blending allows winemakers to fine-tune the different wine components, which is very beneficial for the end product. The marriage of varieties is a high winemaking art that has absolutely nothing to do with mindless mixing, or even dishonest adulteration.

Apart from that, this type of red wine is ideal for lavishly laid tables and culinary circles. Interestingly, these red wines often pair well with very complex dishes. In such alliances, they smooth out taste spikes and, at the same time, gain some finesse. Care should be taken not to serve them too warm, for slightly chilled at 16 degrees Celsius they can adapt easily to any situation.

Red Wine Type 3 🍷🍷🍷
Complex and Elegant

This category makes a connoisseur's heart beat faster. Elegance, brilliance, diversity and complexity are the most desired attributes, and are generally regarded as the highest honor. At the sight of such euphoric wine descriptions some will blankly shake their heads, while others will already have chosen a spot in their cellar for these precious bottles. Ideally, these great finds will be unveiled again only after many years of bottle-age. Only then will they reveal their true class.

Elegance, brilliance, diversity and complexity are particularly desired attributes.

A few decades ago, such high-quality wines emerged mostly by chance, and usually only in exceptional years. Nature determined the result. In addition to an outstanding vineyard and the right grape varieties, the weather during the ripening period had to cooperate. Furthermore, extended bottle aging was necessary for optimal enjoyment. Youthful, awkward wines needed a suitable bottle maturity to smooth out rough tannins and to develop the desired harmony.

Today, the actual quality of a wine is measured in terms of its longevity and potential, which it could not have without perfectly balanced components. The shelf life is, as it were, one of the most important parameters of this particular type of wine. Even for experts, however, it is sometimes difficult to instantly recognize a complex, elegant wine. They are traded at prices between $25–$2,500, and are a sought-after commodity. The trick is to pay as little money as possible for a great wine. Supply, demand and an international trading system determine the price.

Bordeaux has been the champion, with its centuries-old wine-trade system, which worked well in the Middle Ages. At the same time, quality differentiation is becoming blurred. In times of globalization and global warming, Bordeaux is not only producing top-quality wines but also just as many rich, simple, everyday, high-alcohol wines, which makes up the bulk of their wine production. Puristic, elegant and complex wines tend to represent the smallest part of their offering.

This sought-after wine type can be found in almost all European winegrowing areas that have a long-established wine culture and tradition. It makes up only a small percentage of total wine production: Bordeaux and Burgundy top growths; spicy Syrah from the northern Rhône; only a few Reserva and Gran Reserva from Rioja and Ribera del Duero; selected Sangiovese and "Super Tuscans"; and Barolo and Barbaresco, the vanguard of the Italian wine scene. So far, only a few Cabernet Sauvignons from the New World have been able to join this coveted top group, and apart from Bordeaux, only a few blends are represented in this category. All of them come from exceptional vineyard sites, grow in temperate climates, and are carefully aged in oak barrels. The winemakers guide the wine's development extremely light-handedly, and treat these Crus like their own children. When tension and structure blend together with lively acidity, complex fruit flavors, and moderate alcohol to create a wine with a delicious length, it is justifiably declared "high quality."

Red Wine Type 4 🍷🍷🍷🍷
Powerful and Opulent

In southern and particularly warm growing regions, grapes ripen much faster. Acid concentration falls and, in turn, sweetness develops in the form of sugar. Sugar is then converted to alcohol during the subsequent fermentation, which, in a dry wine, leads to a higher alcohol content and, thus, a more full-bodied taste. The origin of such lush, ripe and warm wine types could be in the southern Rhône, where very old, gnarly vines have driven their roots deep into the barren soil. In this region, grapes are virtually baked in the sun, leading to wines which taste pleasantly jammy, spicy, warm and soft.

The intense aromas and flavors remind one of overripe fruits; stewed plum compote with a hint of cinnamon; chocolate and licorice. And because of their high sugar concentration, they seem almost sweet.

This wine type didn't attain cult-status until the 1990s, when juicy, big, red wines of the New World entered the scene. An unprecedented abundance of pleasantly rich fruit aromas jumped out of the glass and quickly took on the European palate which, up until this time, was accustomed to more tannic wines. Before one was aware of the satiating effect of these wines, its alcohol had already numbed their senses. Compared to the familiar, rather acidic and, in their youth, tannic European red wines which first required some years of bottle-age before they could be enjoyed, these fruity blockbusters made a huge impact on the wine world's hitherto clearly-structured standard of taste. Today the new and old wine worlds have converged, both sides benefiting from their respective developments. Lusciously fruity, higher-alcohol wines are now emerging–certainly facilitated by climate change–even in Europe, and can be found, for example, in the Iberian Peninsula, in southern France, Italy and Greece. In the new wine world, aspirations are now moving away from opulence, and heading toward elegance. If possible, vintners now plant their vines in higher, cooler elevations where acidity is retained. Not infrequently, these vineyards are located in extremely high altitudes; for example, in the Argentine Andes at 1,500 meters (4,921 feet) or more above sea level.

By virtue of the often-times very high alcohol content of this rich wine type, its impact is immediate. These concentrated wines may be, on first sip, ever so enjoyable. After the first glass, however, a certain satiation is reached. Therefore, such highly aromatic solo-entertainers must be carefully chosen when pairing with food. A high-alcohol wine with fruity sweetness should be well-incorporated into the meal; for example, a jammy, wonderfully opulent Shiraz easily assumes the role of the cranberries when paired with game. Dark sauces refined with foie gras pair very well with rich, red wine, which, because of its explosive fruit aromas, gives the dish a finishing touch. Also giblets; extremely spicy ingredients; and dishes with an adequate acid structure–for example, marinated kidneys or meat with barbecue sauce–are well-suited because the acidity stands up to these fruity musclemen, and thus allows the appetizing enjoyment to begin.

Sparkling Wine Type 1 🍷
Light and Fresh

This is the category for refreshing, mainly semi-sparkling, wines such as Frizzante and a broad range of branded Sekts. In general, these are industrially produced sparkling wines which are uncomplicated, bubbly, straightforward types that attract a broad audience. They appear in great number on supermarket and discount-store shelves. Everybody's darling, indestructible Prosecco is the true prototype of this genre. With the names Perlwein or Frizzante we are talking about semi-sparkling wines which have a minimum of 8.5 percent alcohol by volume, and a carbon dioxide pressure of up to 2.5 bar. Proper, fully sparkling wine must have a minimum of 3.5 bar. Frizzante and Perlwein also have a different outward appearance than sparkling wine. Due to the high internal pressure, the corks for sparkling wine and Champagne bottles are designed differently. Additionally, the mushroom-shaped cork is held by a four-sided wire mesh clasp to tightly hold the cork on the bottle.

The necessary secondary fermentation, which transports the still wine into its bubbly existence, is usually done in a large tank, in the case of value-priced sparkling wines. Branded Sekts are blended, and are characterized by their consistent taste profiles, regardless of the quality of the vintage. They frequently reach a turnover of several million bottles per year. For this reason alone, base wines for this type of sparkling wine are usually not purchased from dedicated winemakers or individual vineyard sites.

Sparkling Wine Type 2 🍷🍷
Fruity and Harmonious

Champagne is undoubtedly the force behind this category. It was in this region, as long ago as the 17th century, that resourceful, epicurean monks paved the way for "Méthode Champenoise." This method has been painstakingly perfected over the last few centuries and has given Champagne an unparalleled global status. An important feature of a sparkling wine is the secondary fermentation. It is induced by the addition of yeast and takes place–according to the standard in Champagne–in the bottle. However, the law dictates that

the traditional term "Méthode Champenoise" is only allowed to be used in the Champagne region. All other regions and countries can designate this same method—the secondary fermentation in the bottle—alternatively as the "traditional method." Champagne is still the "Mother of All" luxury sparklers, but other regions are closing in on this delicacy. Even top-quality examples of its little brother, Crémant, can be keen competition for any cheap Champagne. England and North America are showing clear ambitions as well. In Germany, these high-quality sparkling wines are called Winzersekt (a vintner's own sparkling wine), in Styria, the formerly acidic Schilcher has evolved into a real delicacy, and even on the other side of the equator Champagne houses have established overseas subsidiaries. An emerging region can be found in the southern part of Brazil where, due to the special geo-climatic situation in the Serra Gaúcha "Vale dos Vinhedos," almost perfect conditions for sparkling wine prevail. The Franciacorta region—which produces Italy's top Spumante as well as Spanish Cava, which is now showing its multifaceted and immense potential—is, next to France, the world's second most important market for bottle-fermented sparkling wine. The range of qualities is, unfortunately, extremely broad in this category. Long-established wineries and quality-driven cooperatives generally offer a much greater potential for real sparkling revelations than large, prestigious brands.

Sparkling Wine Type 3 ♉♉♉
Complex and Elegant

Anyone who has sipped a multi-layered and complex Vintage Champagne knows how stunningly elegant it can taste. In contrast to a still wine, this luxury beverage is interwoven with silky, sparkling bubbles which instantaneously lend wings to its delicious taste. Its only problem is the price. For many, the cost prohibits this sublime pleasure from the outset or, at least, it limits it to a few really special occasions.

Sparkling elegance paired with multilayered substance

Following the méthode champenoise, Champagne can be stored for decades, in constant contact with its youth-preserving yeast, in maze-like chalk cellars. The yeast cells preserve and impart unique, creamy flavors. Vintage Champagnes are the flagship products of all Champagne houses and mature for several years. It is a matter of course that only the very best base wines are used to make Vintage Champagne. In this category there is another, key distinctive feature in the production process: the use of wood. Those Champagne houses which use wood barrels for primary fermentation and subsequent storage of their still wine, tend to use a higher proportion of Pinot Noir grapes in the future cuvée. Champagne made from white grapes usually goes through its primary fermentation in neutral vessels. Some houses–such as Bollinger, Egly-Ouriet, Laval and Krug–use small, oak barrels, while other producers–such as Jacquesson, Roederer and Bedel–prefer to use traditional wood casks. Often, these barriques have an average age of just over 30 years, and the large wood casks are sometimes even older. In Champagne production, an oaky flavor, which is imparted by new oak barrels, is not desired. Instead, the aim is to achieve a touch of toastiness and subtle, caramel-like, nutty flavors that, when they interact, elegantly surround the delicate, fruity flavors. This is pure elegance, combined with powerful substance.

Sparkling Wine Type 4 🍷🍷🍷🍷
Powerful and Opulent

Those who like their bubbles sweet and sumptuous will be well-served with this category. These sparkling wines are made expressly for opulent and sweet enjoyment. Since carbon dioxide strongly attenuates the sensory sweetness in sparkling wine, the residual sugar levels can be much higher than in still wine, without seeming cloying and sticky. Residual sugar levels between 32 and 50 grams per liter–and sometimes even above 50 grams–are not uncommon.

A Crimean sparkling wine made from red or white grapes, with about 80 grams per liter of residual sugar, tastes heavily sweet, while an Australian Sparkling Shiraz with just 40 grams per liter contains a similar sweetness. This intense, red sparkling wine has a seductive, chocolaty cassis aroma and a noticeable tannic structure which, in the case of high-quality examples, can also stem from wood-barrel aging.

Sweet Wine Type 1 🍷
Light and Fresh

Wine types of this category are like a fleeting encounter. One doesn't really notice them for their complexity at first glance. They taste deliciously. These simple and, at the same time, delicate lightweights get by without expansive creaminess and body, with a wonderfully low alcohol content of 7 to 10 percent. The best examples have delicate flavors; a finely chiseled minerality; and a soft, fruit sweetness supported by a lively acidity. These are uncomplicated and delicate lightweights.

Prototypes for this category are Riesling Kabinett wines from the northern German growing regions of Mosel, Saar, Ruwer, Mittelrhein, Nahe and Rheingau, which thrive on stony soils rich in slate. Unfortunately, these light, off-dry wines have been somewhat forgotten as a result of the dry wine trend of the past few decades. In their youth, Kabinett wines are incredibly stimulating and make you want another glass. Actually, you won't want to stop, once you've really had a proper taste of this refreshing delicacy. After several years of bottle age, these Kabinett wines reveal another talent: They evolve into completely under-rated eating companions. One could probably characterize the fizzy Moscato d'Asti as one of the very few extraordinary exceptions in this category. It also thrives on its fruity freshness but belongs, due to its carbon dioxide, in the group of sparkling wines—a wine group to which it legally cannot be assigned due to its low alcohol content (4.5 to 6.5 percent by volume).

Sweet Wine Type 2 🍷🍷
Fruity and Harmonious

In the case of this wine type, the balance between stimulating fruit; juicy acidity; and supporting sweetness determines the quality of its taste. Just like an overly fatty sauce, sticky sweet wines taste terribly boring, because the stimulating support of fresh acidity is lacking. The flavor spectrum of this wine type goes from boringly sweet to exhilaratingly drinkable. This has nothing to do with the levels of sweetness, but with well-balanced fruit, acidity and sweetness. These wines attain a fruity richness from their own

fructose, as a result of stopping fermentation before dryness. Such naturally sweet wines taste much more elegant than those wines whose sweetness is fine-tuned with rectified concentrated grape juice (also known as sweet reserve) and never lose their slightly sugary character. The names Spätlese, Vendange Tardive, Late Harvest and Recioto therefore don't provide a quality orientation, but simply denote a certain level of grape maturity. Spätlese wines, which display a high level of finesse, can easily be classed with the elegant, sweet wine type 3. It is therefore important to not only know the wine, but also know the intentions of the winemaker. The wide range of essential aromas, together with the acid and sugar content, produce the desired flavor explosion in your mouth.

They're formed only after a long growing season in the last sunny days of autumn. Wines from cooler regions have home advantage, and are therefore clearly in the lead.

Sweet Wine Type 3 ♉♉♉
Complex and Elegant

This wine's definite strength lies in the extremely appealing tension between delicious fruit sweetness and lively acidity. Ideally, to achieve this, the grapes are harvested at the peak of their physiological ripeness. A more luxurious style of this wine type emerges when the botrytis cinerea fungus does its insidious handiwork, creating small holes in the skins, thereby slowly dehydrating the grape. This results in a natural concentration of sugars and other components. For the winemaker, this is a delicate balancing act between desirable noble rot and undesirable musty gray mold, which can develop very rapidly when rain and warm temperatures occur at this stage of maturity.

Botrytized (noble-rot-infected) grapes therefore flourish in dry, mostly cool autumn weather with gently warming sunshine. Only then can they shrivel under healthy conditions, and build up the desired concentration. Noble sweet wines exist all over the world, but the truly elegant classics with a high level of complexity are achieved primarily in the northern growing regions of Germany, Loire, Jurançon, Hungary, Austria and Canada. The more acidic Riesling, Chenin Blanc, Petit Maseng, Furmint, Welschriesling and Scheurebe are high on a winemaker's wish list. For most wines, a painstaking manual grape-selection in several passes is necessary. Since the grapes are not always uniformly affected by noble rot, the suitable parts have to be individually selected or broken out (an Austrian style known as "Ruster Ausbruch"). Despite their immense sweetness, these grapes have an incomparably brilliant taste due to their fine acidity.

A particular version of this wine type is found in the ice wines of Germany, Austria, Luxembourg and Canada, in which water freezes out at temperatures below 7 degrees Celsius, leading to the desired concentration. However, since only healthy grapes survive the sometimes unbearably long wait until the end of November, or even into January of the next year, these wines are characterized by an varietally typical fruit expression, and tremendous tension between sweetness and acidity.

Sweet Wine
Type 4 🍷🍷🍷🍷
Powerful and Opulent

With an alcohol level of more than 13 percent by volume, this rich, mostly barrique-aged wine type is exactly the opposite of the multifaceted, brilliant, noble sweet white wines. To produce this thick, almost oily wine type, grapes ripen predominantly on the vine to reach an optimal maturity. Specialties within this category are made from grapes which have been spread out on reed or straw mats to dry. The botrytis, and the resultant extremely high sugar-content, make for a concentration of aromas.

In order to give these wines more structure, these specialties are often aged in small, oak barrels. The wood consumes and masks the alcohol, and transmits gentle, bitter components into the wine, which replaces the missing acidity. They are essential for balancing the flavors of these massive wines and also give the necessary structure. They are accompanied by tantalizing aromas of dried apricot, orange peel, quince, raisins, honey and nuts. This category of noble sweet wine encompasses all other wines which come from southern regions and are made from low-acid varieties.

Fortified Wines ♈-♈♈♈

Fortified wines have fascinating personalities and offer, depending on their country of origin and style, extremely fascinating discoveries. Actually, an entire book should be devoted to this category, because its multiple variations are impossible to lump together in a single category. There is only one common denominator: all of these wines are fortified, which means that at some stage during production, all of them have had high-proof alcohol (ethanol) added to them. If this happens during fermentation, the yeasts which are responsible for fermentation die off, and the natural sweetness of the grapes is preserved in the wine. Exemplary of this are all Vin Doux Naturel wines such as Banyuls, Maury, Muscat de Rivesaltes and Muscat de Beaumes de Venise, as well as opulently sweet Muscats from the New World, Malaga, Madeira and all port wines.

Quite a crucial determinant for the final taste is the time when the alcohol is added, which can vary depending on the product, type, style, and producer. If the wines are fortified at the end of, or after, fermentation, then the result is a rather dry wine type such as Manzanilla; Fino and Amontillado sherries; or Madeira Sercial.

Due to their high alcohol content, these wines receive very little attention in this day and age. Furthermore, sweetness often disguises a lack of finesse, and the consumer will quickly lose interest in this actually exciting wine genre. Port and Madeira can be found for less than $6. These simple, sugary liquids will never, even remotely, evoke the same delicious enchantment as an artisan-made port, sherry or Madeira does.

To be able to properly match fortified wines with food, one should know the main ingredients. The alcohol is stated on the label–but what about the sensory sweetness and the corresponding residual sugar level? The sweetness level of fortified wines influences the taste of sweet or salty foods, while its high alcohol content reacts more with fat and bitter foods. In addition, basic knowledge about other flavor impacts is quite helpful (e.g. fruit flavors, aromas, barrel influence, oxidative or reductive winemaking).

Banyuls and Maury usually range from 45-55 grams of sugar, while Muscat de Rivesaltes has at least 100 and Muscat de Beaumes de Venise has at least 110 grams of sugar per liter. Port wine, depending on the intention

of the winemaker, levels out at 70-95 grams.
Madeira brings forth 20-65 grams for
the drier style Sercial; 50-80 grams for
Verdelho; Bual at 70-95; and Malmsey
starts at around 96 grams per liter. The
situation is very different with sherry:
dry styles can start with about 5 grams, while
the syrupy Pedro Ximenez, in its highly
concentrated form, can boast
more than 350 grams per liter.
These figures are merely indicatory
averages. These can–contingent upon
individual producers–certainly vary.

Mature Wines

Unlike the early days, when wines were allowed to mature, wines are now drunk fairly young. This is due to the change in lifestyle, a faster-moving environment and economic factors. At the same time, modern cellar technology enables earlier stabilization and filtration, whereas prior to this, time was indispensable for these processes. Wines are, therefore, more likely purchased for early consumption, instead of for cellaring. This change in drinking habits has meant that, today, wines are usually drunk young, fresh and fruity. Aged notes are much less appreciated, and even perceived as unpleasant.

Unfortunately, these aged tertiary aromas–such as honey, petroleum, leaves, dried fruit, orange peel and nuts–are lost on many consumers. This is all the more regrettable, because mature wines pair much better with a variety of foods, balancing the flavor differences between dishes with its maturity.

The better the wine quality, the more favorable the conditions for a long cellaring period. After the restless days of youth, many young wines fall into a deep sleep to wake up radiant after one to three years, and then gradually enter into a slow, decomposing phase of maturity. This cycle evolves, depending on the quality, into shorter or longer periods. The natural carbon dioxide, which is a fermentation by-product, gradually disappears. The fresh primary fruit and fermentation aromas in the wine's acidic environment are eliminated, while the minerality, interestingly enough, doesn't change. With increasing oxidation, aged firn notes emerge with mature honey notes; a certain nuttiness; bitter orange peel; apple; and dried-fruit aromas. The wine loses its voluminous mouth-feel and appears much lighter overall. In this case, it is important for a dry wine to have a relatively high level of extract, because the wine's flavor-carrying components, sweetness, and alcohol, diminish sensorially as the wine matures. In light wines, sweetness takes the place of alcohol and it tastes less intense with age, while the sensory perception of acidity increases, causing the wines to appear almost dry without actually being so. A mature, red wine's distinguishing astringency and bitter tannins change positively with age. On the whole, sweetness, acidity and alcohol become very well-integrated, fade sensorially into the background, and release a provocative richness. Young wines, however, are the exact opposite:

their fresh fruit is often joined by a lively acidity, which can make these wines too nervous and edgy to be an optimal food match. Similarly, in young wines, a high level of alcohol can be uncomfortably dominant, and the seemingly superficial sweetness is, at first, irritating. Aged wines are simply stronger and clearer in their taste expression. The ingredients grow together into a flavorful harmony, which co-operate especially well with multifaceted dishes.

Which Glass for Which Wine?

Wine Type Meets Glass Type

What characterizes a good wine glass? Do we really need a special wine glass for each grape variety–something glass manufacturers have long made us believe is true? Is it enough to just know the grape variety in order to be able to determine the wine's taste, character and type?

Pinot Noir, for example, comes in completely different styles and qualities: from ordinary, simple, light, refreshing and fruity to elegant, complex, oak-influenced, powerful and opulent. When we consider varieties such as Riesling and Chenin Blanc, the repertoire of styles varies from dry and medium-dry to sweet. How can one glass adequately cope with all of them? Since the late 1980s, when the first grape varietal glass-collection–with an advanced, sensory improved glass-shape–came on the market, there haven't been, from a functional standpoint, any revolutionary changes. Even so, new wine-glass series continue to come onto the market in a variety of forms and even fashions, including wine-tasting glasses with dual-curved rims. In terms of product quality, on the other hand, there have been notable innovations, such as TRITAN ® crystal glass from Zwiesel Kristallglas and the special surface-coating Drop-Protect, which prevents wine from dripping on the outer edge of the glass.

Some Good Insight

By now you've probably reached the point at which you ask yourself what real purpose a wine glass really has, if it's not just to give you something with which to toast. It has an organoleptic purpose, of course; it is very crucial for appearance, taste and smell. It also has a tactile sensation, temperature and, above all, functionality. A functional glass should first and foremost be wine-friendly.

Dissecting a Wine Glass What constitutes a wine glass' functionality?		
	Details	**Functionality**
	Glass rim	The rim's glass thickness and radius determines the degree of intensity, and the point on which the wine first touches the tongue and its taste zones. If the glass edge bulges out with a rolled rim, then wines will appear short and acidic, while a finely cut, thin rim will allow wine to flow more smoothly onto the tongue. German wine connoisseurs cheekily call a Riesling glass' outwardly curved rim a "Säurespoiler," which translates into "acidity spoiler."
	Bowl length	Since the mouth and throat are connected with the olfactory nerves, tasting and smelling occur at the same time. The width of the bowl as well as its length (from the bottom of the glass bowl to the rim) have an impact on the aroma intensity.
	Bowl form	The goblet should be tapered up to the top in an egg-shaped form in order to capture and hold the aromas, and to provide sufficient capacity for the wine so it doesn't swish out when it's being swirled. The bowl-width is critical for the evaporation surface area. The wider the glass, the more wine can be impacted by oxygen, and the quicker the developing aroma molecules can rise up.
	Stem	Prevents unattractive fingerprints on the bowl, as well as an unnecessary increase in wine temperature from warm hands and fingers.
	Tactile sensation	This is about the active tactile perception of size, contour, surface texture, weight, and balance of an object. This applies to both the glass and its contents. For this, your sense of touch is used through the integration of skin sensors. The tactile sensations make sure that the brain can identify, locate and evaluate mechanical stimuli, temperature, viscosity, and also pain.

Conclusion

The Viña wine glass serves as an example for a practical, everyday universal glass; an "all-rounder" which can be found in almost every glass series. The variable wine components such as "fruit, acidity, tannin and alcohol" are transported well in this glass and, due to its functionality, they can be tasted with a significant degree of objectivity.

Basic Inventory
Which glass for which wine?

	Type 1 Light and Fresh	Type 2 Fruity and Harmonious	Type 3 Complex and Elegant	Type 4 Powerful and Opulent
	Light, lean wine, usually vinified in stainless steel. Clear aromas, lives from its acidity and fruit, and—when it originates from warm or hot regions—from its youthfulness.	Medium-bodied wine with smooth texture, fresh-to-spicy ripe aromas, medium intensity. Moderate, mild-to-juicy acidity, harmonious.	Multilayered, elegant wine, without oak or with perfectly integrated oak. Lively, clearly defined, and integrated acidity. Complex aromas, structure and length.	Juicy, opulent and full-bodied, powerful structure, detectable alcohol. Without oak, but also with considerable oak influence. Ripe and expansive, low acidity, sometimes over-ripe and lusciously fat.
All-rounder 	The glass supports these light, fresh wine types. The small capacity and slender bowl lead the aromas, even with small pours, directly to the nose.	Supports this medium-bodied, fruity and harmonious wine type, brings the aromas positively to the fore.	The wine already reveals everything it has to offer, complexity and multiple layers are perceptible. It could, however, certainly benefit from a larger glass.	The wine shows off its powerful opulence, however it needs a slightly larger glass for it to better reveal its intense aromatics.
Burgundy Glass 	This delicate, rather light wine type has little chance in this bulbous glass. It literally vanishes in the large and bulbous bowl.	Depending on the intensity, this fruity and harmonious wine type is at home in this bulbous glass. The glass is, however, too bulbous for its somewhat lighter relatives; its aromas escape too quickly.	Young, deep, but also somewhat more complex and elegant wine types need oxygen in order to evolve. For this reason, the bowl should be more bulbous, and also provide a larger surface. Additionally, the opening should be larger.	This glass supports the aromas of barrique-aged white and red wines, provided they have enough acidity and aren't too alcoholic. The same is true for fuller-bodied sweet wines with a good corresponding acidity. If the wine lacks lively acidity, then the alcohol can rise unpleasantly into the nose.
Bordeaux Glass 	This delicate, light wine type's odds are limited in this Bordeaux glass. Exceptions to this rule could possibly be made for certain, more expressive red wine types.	Depending on its intensity, this juicy and harmonious wine type can be at home in this large glass with a high bowl. However, it can prove to be difficult for the lighter wine types in this category.	Wine types with integrated, more moderate acidity, intense aromas and tannins need a large glass with a long bowl in order to perfectly present their multilayered elegance.	Powerful, opulent and also higher alcohol wines with low acidity are best enjoyed in a large glass with a long bowl. In this glass, the wine's opulence is slightly throttled and appears somewhat more elegant in the nose and on the palate.

Experiment:

For this experiment you will need five pre-specified wine glasses (see the table on page 87), and one bottle of wine per wine type for four to five people. Depending on the size of each glass, pour between 2-5cl. Those who are interested in this experiment should first search in their own cupboards for the right glasses. Otherwise, almost all types of glasses, including matching wines, can be purchased directly in the Zwiesel Kristallglas Shop **(www.zwieselkristall-glas-shop.com)**.

One for All

Fruit, acidity, tannin and alcohol are the variable components of a wine whose perception can be influenced significantly by the glass. There is no single glass that meets all requirements perfectly, therefore one must be prepared to compromise. There are practical all-rounders–everyday, universal glasses from which you can taste almost any wine without hesitation–which do not cause the sensory relationships between wine components to change very much. But when it comes to true enjoyment and the optimal development of a complex wine, the universal glass is no longer sufficient. To convey the multifaceted aromas, flavors and textures of such a wine, you should use a glass which corresponds to the type of wine.

Less is More

The trade offers a wide variety of glass types, but for a good, basic assortment you can be very well-served with a manageable range of glass types. Do not worry, you need not banish your favorite glass. You should base your choices on your personal preference, as long as there is respect for the functionality of the glass. It is simply and solely the wine, not the grape variety or even the glass design, which determines the requisite glass shape or the ideal shape of the bowl.

Which Wine from Which Glass?

The wrong wine glass can have a negative impact on a wine. Good wine glasses are, therefore, indispensable tools for a high-quality drinking experience. What should be considered isn't just the price of the glasses, but also their form and workmanship. The following experiment will prove that the same wine can taste completely different in different glasses. Test it out for yourself. After that, you'll know which glass goes with which type of wine.

How does one wine type taste from different glasses?

White Wine Type 4 Powerful and Opulent 2010 Chardonnay Barrel Fermented, Jordan, Stellenbosch, South Africa

Tasting Glass IDEAL / INAO

Smell: Smoky, tangy, almost spicy, fruit is in the background, oak notes are emphasized, lacks charm.
Taste: At first, sweet, vanilla aromas, then oak-dominant and acidic. Medium-bodied, alcohol is emphasized. Lacks elegance and complexity.
Finish: Bitter, short, tangy grapefruit notes, the alcohol lingers.
Conclusion: This glass has a tasting-glass character, small, short-stem, somewhat basic, fingers touch the bowl, fine but relatively narrow. During drinking the nose is above the glass rim, the impact on the wine is, in this case, negative.

Wine Glass BISTRO

Smell: Little fruit, oak influence is perceptible, smoky, tangy, somewhat spicy, all-in-all somewhat restrained and lacking charm.
Taste: Sweet-sour, some vanilla, oak-emphasized and lemony notes. Medium-bodied, alcohol is emphasized, lacks elegance and complexity.
Finish: Bitter, grapefruit and sour citrus flavors, short and one-dimensional, alcohol and astringency linger.
Conclusion: Impressions are all-in-all weaker due to the robust glass. Very thick rim which touches the tongue, the tip of the nose touches the glass, because of the thick rim. The wine "plops" onto the middle of the tongue.

Wine Glass VIÑA

Smell: Pleasant, delicately fruity aromas, grapefruit notes, delicate and well-integrated oak influence, all-in-all balanced, lightly smoky, animating.
Taste: Very juicy, pear aromas, pomelo grapefruit, integrated, lively fruit acidity, medium body, refreshing texture.
Finish: Juicy, harmonious acidity and fruitiness, perceptible alcohol but well-integrated, pleasant length and depth.
Conclusion: As if another wine were in the glass. In comparison, much fruitier aromas. The glass is appealing and well-balanced. Fine rim, thin stem, optimally formed bowl, and well-proportioned bowl length, allows the fruit aromas to come to the fore.

Burgundy Glass VIÑA

Smell: At first restrained, slightly dusty, delicately fruity, vanilla notes, pear, pomelo grapefruit, complex.
Taste: Stimulating, juicy acidity, ripe yellow fruits, pear, pineapple, lots of depth, multilayered, pleasantly creamy. Alcohol is well-integrated, complex and juicy, pleasant texture.
Finish: Fruit dominant, a certain elegance, smooth acidity, opulent length, perceptible alcohol, lots of depth and texture.
Conclusion: Very pleasing glass, balanced despite the large bowl. Larger surface provides for increased oxygen contact, optimally scaled bowl length, which transports the aromas carefully, yet in all its facets, toward the nose.

Bordeaux Glass VIÑA

Smell: Slightly dusty, fruit restrained, bitter grapefruit aromas, citrus, overall one-dimensional, oak is hardly perceptible.
Taste: Soft, full-flavored, lacks sophistication, mostly rich, broad, vanilla, its brief juiciness turns alcoholic and bitter, astringent roughness. Oak impression is cedary and not integrated.
Finish: Alcohol becomes dominant and covers up all other aromas, leaving a citrus-like acidity.
Conclusion: This glass is tactually pleasing and balanced, with a high and wide bowl. Aromas have a long way to travel to the nose. The glass doesn't provide enough surface in the center, which subdues the aromas and unpleasantly emphasizes the alcohol and acidity.

A Systematic
Approach to Food

A Foray into Food

What Matters

After the chapter on systematic wine enjoyment follows an outline of the different foods, their components and their preparation methods. Basic product and cooking knowledge, as well as the appropriate food chemistry background are essential and beneficial for this discussion. Practical insight into the combination of wine and food will be explored systematically.

At the outset we are faced with a mountain of questions: Which wine components are compatible with which of the dish's ingredients, and which ones lead to surprising synergies? What reactions are triggered by which stimuli? How do different cooking methods change an ingredient's flavor? Why is it much harder to perceptibly change a layer of fat which coats the palate than to influence the intensity of salt, sweetness, acidity and bitterness.

Who with Whom?

In our search for the answer to the most important questions, we will focus first on the food's ingredients, and then gradually work out a basic framework for a system of combinations. In addition to presenting some culinary experiments, the essential rules for a successful combination of wine and food are addressed.

Maintain an Overall View

The summary in table form (see page 100) should serve, without any long explanations, as a first orientation and an easy-to-read checklist.

Know the Drill

In the next step, you'll further develop your ability to combine food and wine, which will be gradually honed by a wealth of delicious experiences you'll collect over the course of time. For the simple reason that it is a very enjoyable task, you will voluntarily practice on a regular basis: eating, drinking and, most particularly, pairing. Well, you'll have to try out for yourself whether the chemistry is really right, and then follow your taste! And, please, never forget that there is neither a universal taste nor a universal flavor combination. Thank goodness!

These Components Are Important:

WINE	FOOD
Flavors	Flavors
Acidity	Acidity
Sweetness	Carbohydrates, Sweetness
Minerals (extracts)	Minerals (salts)
Phenols	Roasted aromas
	Protein/Amino acids
Alcohol/Ethanol	Fat

This comparative table shows that wine and food are very similar in their components with the exception of protein, which doesn't have a direct counterpart in wine. This is a good reason for examining protein and its effects very carefully. Of prime importance are the reciprocal interactions of these individual components.

Every human being collects a kind of "library of flavors" in the course of his or her life that remains in his memory. The better the sensory skills are trained, the easier it is to recognize aroma impressions and analyze unfamiliar flavors.

Flavors Flavors are separate chemical compounds or compositions, and are characterized by the combination of a specific smell and individual taste. Flavor perception is first determined by aromas and fragrances. These aroma molecules (soluble in water, fat or alcohol) are released during the action of chewing and swallowing. They reach the olfactory receptors in the nose via a detour through the posterior pharynx. Here, they compete with each other and can complement or overlap one another.

Acids are perceived in different intensities, depending on their concentration. Lemon juice, for example, is able to break down the protein in meat or fish. To make this dish compatible with wine, an offsetting buffer of salt should be added, because it absorbs the acid and pushes the fruit flavors to the fore (known as "The Tequila Effect.").

Acid Both in wine and in food, the taste characteristics of acid cannot be ignored. A wine's acidity depends primarily on grape variety, growing region, vintage, time of harvest and winemaking technology, and can, therefore, be present in varying amounts. A wine's total acidity is usually between 4 and 10 grams per liter. Red wine has, on average, a lower total acidity than white wine. In food, one can distinguish between direct and indirect acidity sources. The indirect sources (meat, fish, poultry, game, fresh cheese, meat and broth) deliver a surplus of acidic minerals and have a delayed or subtle effect. The direct (vinegar, lemon, citrus fruits, sour-tasting fruit, and lactic-acid-fermented vegetables such as sauerkraut) have an immediate effect.

Sweetness Sugar in wine consists mainly of glucose and fructose. A food's sweet taste-impression not only results from the addition of sugar, but also from other carbohydrates. Dense, viscous liquids or sauces that contain fat can also be perceived by our brain as being sweet, even though they don't contain sugar. These energy sources, together with fats and proteins, make up the quantitatively largest digestible (starch) and non-digestible (dietary fiber) proportion of our diet. Sweetness, however, always needs the addition of aromas and acidity before its taste can be appreciated. An extra pinch of salt can often tip the scale in order to achieve a perfect balance.

Minerals (Extracts) This is a collective term for many different substances and solids which are present in a dissolved form in wine and, unlike alcohol and aromas, are non-volatile. When sugar, glycerin and acid are removed from wine, what remains are minerals. Boil a small amount of wine until no more liquid is present, and "extract" is what remains. The more minerals a vine absorbs from the soil, the richer the extract found in the future wine becomes. This is an advantage when pairing wine with acid-rich foods, because the wine extracts can buffer the food's acidity due to its concentration of minerals salts.

Minerals (Salts) Salt is used as a seasoning in every type of cuisine. It consists mainly of sodium chloride, and contains up to three percent of other salts and additional substances. Everyone recognizes the taste of salt. Most everyone has experienced the range of flavors and effects of salt: pleasant and stimulating, to unbearably salty and sharp. The taste of a dish can be influenced, to a great extent, by the addition of just a pinch of salt. When combined with some acids, such as lemon juice or vinegar, salt can actually be used as a positive, manipulative element as a way to create a harmonious connection to wine. Salt is a powerful flavor-enhancer, which has a positive effect on wine in general.

Phenols In wine, there are hundreds of different phytochemicals, which are grouped under the umbrella term "polyphenols." During the winemaking process, they go from the grape skins, pulp, stems and seeds into the grape juice. These phytochemicals include tannins, red anthocyanins, and numerous phenolic compounds. The wine's astringent, slightly bitter characteristics ultimately depend on the grape variety, soil and growing conditions, as well as on the production and fermentation techniques.

An oak barrel can give the wine an intense, roasted taste due to the toasting of the barrel's interior.

Roasted Flavors Under strong exposure to heat, compounds made up of proteins and reduced sugars responsible for browning and caramel-like taste are generated on the surfaces of roasted foods. Thus, an aromatic crust (Maillard reaction) is formed which possesses astringent, caramelized, and lightly bitter, roasted flavors.

Alcohol Alcohol is created by the fermentation of sugar. The alcohol content of wine is usually between 9 and 14 percent. There are exceptions to these rules, however: the alcohol content of Italian Moscato d'Asti, or of German Trockenbeerenauslese is often less than 8.5 percent, while that of fortified wines (port or sherry, for example) is well over 15 percent. Alcohol can dissolve flavor, and is therefore an important flavor-carrier in wine. Wines with a high alcohol-content also contain greater amounts of glycerol, a higher-quality alcohol which can make wine taste fuller, softer and creamier. Just like fat in food, alcohol enhances the flavors, as well as all other sensory perceptions.

Fat is in a position to manipulate all the other flavors positively or negatively. Molecules can be dissolved in fat, alcohol or water. While the basic tastes of sweet, sour, salty and umami are all water soluble, this quality applies to bitter tastes only under certain conditions.

Fat Fats are found in the tissues of fish and meat, milk, and plant parts. In general, they are odorless and tasteless, and have a flavor-enhancing effect similar to alcohol. Many flavors dissolve only in fat. On a tactile level, fat makes its presence felt through a creamy mouth-feel. Flavor molecules move into, and are captured in, the respective fat, oil or butter, and are then distributed across the tongue. Volatile essential oils can, for example, be trapped in the oil droplets of an emulsion where their taste takes effect.

So, a food or dish that contains fat tastes better, or more intense, because fat can dissolve considerably more flavor-determining substances. Since there are many different types of fat, the flavor impact can vary greatly depending on the fat content. Unsaturated fatty acids (e.g., vegetable oil, olive oil and fish) bring about a pleasantly creamy and stimulating mouth-feel, while saturated fats (e.g., animal fat, meat, cream and butter) tend to leave a thick coating-impression on the palate. This taste impression can be changed, and almost neutralized through the careful addition of salt; acid (lemon juice or vinegar); and spice. The tongue's receptors perceive the sensations of "hot" or "spicy," and stimulate the brain's trigeminal nerve–much in the way it perceives astringent sensations from the tannins found in wine. The pain-inducing molecules of pepper, chili and ginger are, just like tannins, predominantly soluble in alcohol or fat. Good examples are chili oil or chocolate aromatized with peppercorns and chili.

Protein (in milk products) The four main components of milk products are fat; protein; minerals (especially calcium); and water (90 percent). In order not to dive too deeply into the field of food chemistry, we will first only distinguish between low-fat dairy products (e.g., yogurt and low-fat cottage cheese) and high-fat dairy products (e.g., cream, crème fraîche and crème double).

Protein (from soy beans) Protein that is extracted from soy beans is an essential nutrient. It is especially important to vegans; soy protein contains amino acids, which are otherwise found only in animal protein.

Protein (in fish and meat) Protein is also present in the muscle and connective tissue of both fish and meat. To break down the protein found in connective tissue, one can use a variety of cooking methods e.g., braising, cooking, frying and grilling. The respective cooking method splits the long-chained proteins into their basic components. This has an impact on taste, creating a vital flavor link that influences the subsequent choice of wine.

Notes on Proteins

The various cooking and preparation methods are very important, because each one is specifically suited to a particular type of meat or fish. This explains why wine types are paired with cooking methods and not with the meat or fish.

Fish and meat contain actin and myosin, which are muscle proteins, as well as collagen, which is found in the connective tissue. Before they can be consumed, many of these proteins must be split physically (during cooking). Unlike meat, fish has much less connective tissue. Cooking or heat is not necessary to split the proteins in fish and pure muscle meat (e.g., thinly-sliced fillet); and just a little lemon juice (acid) and salt does the job quite well.

Proteins are split into peptides and amino acids. Each amino acid possesses a different flavor substance–lysine is sweet; asparagine has a neutral flavor; and glutamic acid has a savory, or meaty taste. Each individual flavor is only released during cooking or preservation. Amino acids are also able to bind with other substances during the cooking process; for example, they react with sugars to create a new connection and, in so doing, produce an altered taste-impression.

The Proper Preparation Makes the Difference

Different preparation methods originally arose out of the need to make meat palatable.

The choice of cooking method depends on the type of meat, as well as the desired flavor outcome. From a culinary standpoint, a distinction must be made between high-quality cuts of meat that can be fried, grilled, or consumed raw, and meat-cuts that are rich in connective tissue and need to be cooked or stewed for a longer period of time.

An aromatic meat-crust, full of roasted flavors, is formed at temperatures between 150 and 200 degrees Celsius. The conversion of connective tissue and muscle protein into collagen, actin and myosin occurs at about 70 degrees Celsius. In the process, amino acids and reduced sugars are converted into new compounds.

A piece of roasted or grilled meat is considered done when a brown crust forms, and the core temperature reaches 70 degrees Celsius. With tender, short-fibered pieces of meat, however, the optimal core temperature is substantially lower. Advised cooking methods for muscle-meat with little connective tissue (e.g., fillet, loin, rump and topside) include sautéing, roasting, broiling or grilling. With firm, long-fibered cuts of meat, the core cooking temperature must be maintained over a much longer period of time, which is why these cuts should not be sautéed or dry-roasted. The hard collagen absorbs liquid during the cooking process, and is thereby converted into softer-textured gelatin. Braising or poaching–slow and moist cooking methods performed at relatively low temperatures–are recommended for tougher meats rich in connective tissue (e.g., neck and sinew from the shoulder and leg).

Cooking Methods

Roasting and Grilling Roasting is probably the oldest cooking method, because it doesn't require any pots, but simply an open fire. Grilling, oven-roasting or pan-frying are commonly lumped together under the general term "roasting." With these cooking methods, compounds made from proteins and sugar molecules are formed on the surface of the meat. These compounds are responsible for the browning and the typical flavor. This process of browning, the so-called "Maillard Reaction," is named after the chemist Louis-Camille Maillard. The crust is not formed because searing the meat "closes the pores," but because water evaporates on the meat's surface. This way, an aromatic crust with an astringent, slightly bitter, roasted flavor is formed. When grilling or broiling, the roasted flavors are much more pronounced, due to the direct radiation of heat.

Stewing or Braising If liquid is added after the meat is seared, the cooking method is called "braising" or "stewing." This moist method is suitable for cuts of meat with tough connective tissue and/or a high fat-content. The meat becomes wonderfully tender and has (despite its soft consistency) mild, roasted flavors as well as sweet notes.

Boiling Boiling refers to any cooking process performed in boiling liquid. It is suitable for cuts of meat with a very high proportion of connective tissue. The meat becomes tender and soft. With this method, there aren't any roasted aromas so boiled meat requires a broth or sauce in order to transport flavor.

Acid breaks down meat fibers; acts as a preservative; and takes over the role of natural maturation.

Poaching Poaching is a very gentle cooking method performed in a hot, but non-boiling, liquid (i.e. below 100 degrees Celsius, in a bath of stock or water). Also with this method, roasted aromas don't develop. If the food itself is not aromatic enough, it may need some flavor support in the form of a broth, sauce, marinade or tapenade.

Steaming Steaming is a particularly gentle cooking method done with vaporized water. It is more suitable for vegetables and fish.

Marinating A marinade (e.g., a mixture of wine, lemon juice, vinegar, oil, salt and spices) is a fast food-preservative. It imparts a special flavor on raw fish or meat, and transforms its original, firm state into a softer consistency. The acid in a marinade breaks down the connective tissue of the meat. A large piece of meat can be tenderized and softened in a marinade prior to cooking. This can take several days, however, because there is no heat to speed up the marinating process.

Salting Salting is an ancient preservation method used to preserve fish and meat. Salt is used to draw moisture out of the meat. The removal of water takes away the means of subsistence for microorganisms, thereby making the meat less perishable. Pickling is another form of salting. During the pickling process, herbs, spices and lemon peel are commonly added to the salt.

The Physical Variable

Structure and Texture Other factors which influence wine and food pairing are temperature and mouth-feel, which shouldn't be underestimated. The textures of foods and beverages play an important role. Everyone can feel the different viscosities of water and oil, or detect the astringent, dry taste of black tea. A different kind of mouth-feel may arise, for example, from the rich creaminess of soft, fatty elements. A firm, almost rubbery impression, comes from collagen when it takes the form of gelatin. When salt dissolves in water, it will taste salty because it is recognized by the corresponding olfactory receptors as "salty." If salt flakes or fleur de sel is combined with fat, a stimulating culinary creation is the result. This can be a simple slice of bread with salty butter, chocolate with fleur de sel, or a fried fish fillet with crunchy salt flakes. The combination of salt and fat will also cause a sparkling wine's bubbles to tingle on the tongue so unyieldingly, that it can emphasize or manipulate a flavor or aroma.

However, the best-known "texturizer" is the fifth basic taste, "umami" (see page 34). This natural flavor-enhancer is formed by glutamic acid, and is present in foods such as tomato paste, grain and aged parmesan. Umami is also present in soy protein. Umami, in conjunction with salt, provides an intense, savory taste, and a corresponding mouth-feel.

This natural substance, however, is also known as the flavor enhancer glutamate, which is used in disproportionate quantities. Glutamate is present in almost all packaged convenience foods, and is used to replace or increase the flavors in natural, fresh foods.

Temperature Temperature plays an important role in how a food is perceived, in the same way that mouth-feel does. Most people only notice temperature in certain situations, or at extreme levels. Overly chilled food keeps its aromas and flavors hidden, with only astringent tannins coming to the fore, and the cold feeling interferes with all other sensations. Heat intensifies all taste impressions, including the negative ones–for example, alcohol.

	White Wine Type 1 — fresh, fruity, light	White Wine Type 2 — medium-bodied	White Wine Type 3 — complex, elegant	White Wine Type 4 — powerful & opulent	Red Wine Type 1 — fresh, fruity, light	Red Wine Type 2 — medium-bodied	Red Wine Type 3 — complex, elegant	Red Wine Type 4 — powerful & opulent	Sparkling Wine Type 1 — fresh, fruity, light	Sparkling Wine Type 2 — medium-bodied	Sparkling Wine Type 3 — complex, elegant	Sparkling Wine Type 4 — opulent, sweet, broad
low acidity	😊	😊	😊	😊	😊	😊	😊	😊	😊	😊	😊	😊
high acidity	😟	😐	😐	😊	😟	😟	😟	😟	😟	😟	😟	😟
low sweetness	😐	😐	😐	😐	😐	😐	😐	😐	😐	😐	😐	😐
moderately sweet	😟	😐	😐	😟	😟	😐	😐	😟	😊	😊	😐	😐
very sweet	😟	😟	😟	😟	😟	😟	😟	😟	😟	😟	😟	😟
low salt content	😊	😊	😊	😊	😊	😊	😊	😊	😊	😊	😊	😊
salty	😐	😊	😐	😐	😐	😊	😐	😐	😐	😐	😊	😊
very salty	😟	😐	😐	😐	😟	😐	😐	😐	😟	😐	😐	😐
piquant	😐	😐	😐	😐	😐	😐	😐	😐	😊	😐	😐	😊
very spicy	😟	😟	😟	😟	😟	😟	😟	😟	😟	😟	😟	😊
gently bitter	😐	😐	😐	😐	😐	😐	😊	😊	😐	😐	😐	😊
very bitter	😟	😟	😐	😐	😟	😐	😐	😊	😟	😐	😟	😊
low fat	😐	😐	😐	😟	😐	😟	😟	😟	😐	😐	😐	😐
high fat	😟	😐	😐	😊	😐	😊	😊	😊	😊	😊	😊	😊
milk protein, low fat	😟	😟	😟	😟	😟	😟	😟	😟	😟	😟	😟	😟
milk protein, high fat	😟	😐	😐	😊	😐	😐	😐	😐	😐	😐	😐	😐
raw (fish)	😐	😐	😐	😟	😟	😟	😟	😟	😐	😐	😊	😟
raw (meat)	😐	😐	😐	😟	😐	😐	😐	😟	😟	😐	😐	😟
marinated (salt & acidity)	😊	😊	😐	😐	😐	😐	😐	😐	😐	😐	😐	😐
steamed (poached)	😊	😐	😐	😐	😐	😐	😐	😟	😐	😐	😐	😟
cooked	😐	😐	😐	😐	😐	😐	😟	😟	😐	😐	😐	😟
roasted	😐	😊	😐	😊	😐	😐	😐	😐	😐	😐	😐	😐
grilled	😟	😐	😐	😐	😐	😐	😐	😐	😐	😐	😐	😐
braised	😟	😐	😐	😐	😐	😐	😐	😐	😐	😟	😐	😟

😊 Wonderful combination. Wine and dish complement each other.

😐 So-so. Not ideal.

😟 Doesn't work. The wine or dish change for the worse.

	Sweet Wine Type 1 fresh, fruity, light	Sweet Wine Type 2 medium-bodied	Sweet Wine Type 3 complex, elegant	Sweet Wine Type 4 powerful & opulent	Fortified Wine Type 2, dry dry, medium-bodied	Fortified Wine Type 2, sweet dry, medium-bodied	Fortified Wine Type 3, dry complex, elegant	Fortified Wine Type 3, sweet complex, elegant	Fortified Wine Type 4, dry opulent, powerful, expansive	Fortified Wine Type 4, sweet opulent, powerful, expansive
low acidity	😐	🙁	🙁	🙁	😐	🙁	😐	🙁	😐	🙁
high acidity	🙂	🙂	🙂	🙂	😐	🙂	🙂	🙂	😐	🙂
low sweetness	🙂	🙂	🙂	🙂	🙂	🙂	🙂	🙂	🙂	🙂
moderately sweet	😐	😐	😐	😐	😐	🙂	😐	🙂	😐	🙂
very sweet	😐	😐	🙂	🙂	🙁	🙂	🙁	🙂	😐	🙂
low salt content	🙂	🙂	🙂	🙂	🙂	🙂	🙂	🙂	🙂	🙂
salty	🙂	🙂	🙂	🙂	🙂	🙂	🙂	🙂	🙂	🙂
very salty	🙂	🙂	🙂	🙂	🙂	🙂	🙂	🙂	🙂	🙂
piquant	🙂	🙂	🙂	🙂	🙂	🙂	🙂	🙂	🙂	🙂
very spicy	😐	🙂	🙂	🙂	😐	🙂	🙂	😐	🙂	🙂
gently bitter	🙂	🙂	🙂	🙂	🙂	🙂	🙂	🙂	🙂	🙂
very bitter	😐	🙂	🙂	🙂	😐	🙂	😐	🙂	🙂	😐
low fat	🙂	🙂	😐	😐	😐	🙁	😐	🙁	🙁	🙁
high fat	😐	😐	🙂	🙂	😐	🙂	😐	🙂	🙂	🙂
milk protein, low-fat	🙁	🙁	🙁	🙁	🙁	🙁	🙁	🙁	🙁	🙁
milk protein, high-fat	😐	🙂	🙂	🙂	😐	🙂	😐	🙂	🙂	🙂
raw (fish)	😐	🙂	🙂	🙁	🙂	🙁	😐	🙁	🙁	🙁
raw (meat)	😐	😐	😐	🙁	😐	😐	😐	🙁	🙁	🙁
marinated (salt & acidity)	🙂	🙂	🙂	😐	🙂	🙂	🙂	🙂	🙂	😐
steamed (poached)	🙂	😐	😐	😐	😐	🙁	😐	🙁	😐	🙁
cooked	😐	😐	😐	😐	🙂	🙁	😐	🙁	😐	🙁
roasted	🙂	🙂	🙂	🙂	🙂	🙂	🙂	🙂	🙂	🙂
grilled	🙂	🙂	🙂	🙂	🙂	🙂	🙂	🙂	🙂	🙂
braised	😐	😐	😐	😐	😐	😐	😐	😐	😐	🙁

Culinary
Experiments

Culinary Experiments

Instructions for Experimenting on Your Own

In this chapter, you can put your theoretical knowledge into culinary practice. Carrying out your own tests will help you experience, taste and learn the most important rules of wine and food pairing. These culinary experiments use the same main ingredients which have been processed in different ways. What does this mean in practice? What factors influence the combination of wine and food?

Aromas

A delicious alliance can be achieved with similar as well as contrasting aromas and flavors. Because it's much easier to search for parallel or harmonious taste impressions, the following experiments are good exercises for beginners as well as the advanced food and wine pairing aficionado. Of course, it also has to do with combinations in which the tension comes from contrasting flavors. The intense aromas play the main role in almost all experiments. Perhaps it is best to compare flavor intensity with volume control. Are they more fresh or mature? Loud or muted?

Mouthfeel

How does the palate react to saltiness, sweetness, acidity, bitterness, umami, fat and texture? There's a big difference between biting into greasy-but-crispy fries, or biting into soggy ones. Does your palate get coated by sweetness or fat, or is it stimulated by acidity or bitterness?

Preparation

What role does food preparation play? A piece of meat, for example, reacts in different ways depending on whether it is grilled, fried, braised, poached or marinated raw. For example, compare the tastes of cooked and raw onions, or roast beef and carpaccio.

Instructions

The following experiments can be carried out alone. It is much more fun, however, to try them in a spirited group of wine-loving friends. First, try the different wines, describe them and make notes if necessary. Then, try each dish with all the wines. When you do this, figure out how the wines change in combination with food, and which wine pairs best with which dish.

Note:
A wine's flavour changes in combination with food.

Wines

Since the cooking methods and ingredients vary for each dish, there are different requirements for the accompanying wines. For a successful wine and food alliance, it is not so much a question of whether to prepare fish or meat, but rather what cooking method to use; the structure of the ingredients; and the intensity of the spices. All wines in these experiments are listed according to wine type categories, and are therefore interchangeable or can be substituted.

	Dish 1	Dish 2	Dish 3	Dish 4	Dish 5
Wine 1					
Wine 2					
Wine 3					

Advice:
If you lack the right words, use smiley faces instead.

🙂 **Wonderful combination**
(Wine and dish complement each other.)

😐 **So-so**
(Not ideal.)

☹️ **Doesn't work**
(The wine or dish changed for the worse.)

Conclusion

Why must you do this yourself? Because wine and food pairings which you have tried for yourself will be much more deeply ingrained than any theories you have read. While you are experimenting and tasting, you will be filling up your personal libarary with aromas and flavors from which you can recall relevant information when you need it. You will acquire culinary knowledge and helpful rules of thumb with which you can successfully accomplish the art of pairing wine with food.

Everyday Prototypes
For Culinary Experiments

Since we are serving up recipes for culinary experiments, we have referred to the wine type classification (page 48) and have chosen three everyday, well-known, prototypes. From now on, theory will be accompanied by reliable, practical self-tests—an exciting way to train your senses.

White Wine Type 1 🍷 Light and Fresh
2010 Riesling vom Schiefer, Qualitätswein trocken,
Weingut Ansgar Clüsserath, Trittenheim, Mosel, Germany

A fresh Riesling, soothingly light with aromas of peach, green apple and a hint of smoky minerality. This is a perfect introduction to the world of steep-sloped Mosel Riesling. The drinkability and minerality simply whet your appetite for the next sip. With 7.2 grams per liter of residual sugar, this classic slate Riesling is on the dry side. The acid—about 8 grams per liter—is well-integrated. A light wine, with a pleasant depth and delicate structure. Refreshing acidity and soft richness ensure stimulating balance, and give the wine a pursuant length. This Riesling has been classically matured in large, used casks. With its low alcohol level (11.5 percent), it presents itself as a fresh, uncomplicated, everyday wine. Its style is commensurate with a light, quaffable, low-alcohol white wine type.

White Wine Type 4 🍷🍷🍷🍷 Powerful and Opulent
2010 Chardonnay, Jordan, Stellenbosch, South Africa

Chardonnay—barrique-aged, with Burgundy acting as its model—is now produced all over the world. It is available in the full spectrum from elegantly fruity to lushly opulent. During malolactic fermentation (MLF), crisp malic acid is converted into softer, lactic acid. As a result, the wine tastes softer, rounder and on the whole, creamier. Due to the time the wine spends in oak, silky vanilla notes are joined by noticeable oak spice and slightly bitter roasted flavors. With a residual sugar content of about 3 grams per liter, this Chardonnay can be considered dry. The high alcohol content (about 14 percent by volume) is very well-integrated, and brings forth creamy richness. Fruity pineapple notes; a hint of quince jelly; yellow fruits and grapefruit aromas; and invigorating acidity (about 6 grams per liter) lead into a pleasant length with juicy creaminess.

Red Wine Type 2 🍷🍷 Fruity and Harmonious
2010 Gemini II, Birgit Braunstein, Purbach, Neusiedlersee-Hügelland, Austria

This appealing, fruity red wine cuvée is representative of a red wine type that can be found all over the world. The assemblage of this wine is made up of Gamay, Cabernet Sauvignon and Zweigelt. The Cabernet Sauvignon portion is recognizable by the typical cassis note, which is joined by sour cherry and forest-berry notes as well as a gentle cedarwood scent. The medium-bodied, well-balanced Gemini was aged partly in new and partly in used oak barrels for about a year. With a total acidity of about 5.5 grams per liter, and a residual sugar content of about 1 gram per liter, it tastes absolutely dry. The still, somewhat youthful, acidity brings forth a pleasant liveliness, and charmingly surrounds the ripe tannins with juicy fruit. The alcohol of 13 percent is within the moderately light realm, and is well integrated. The juicy fruit-flavors are accompanied by delicate roasted aromas that show length and structure, which suggests good aging potential.

Bread and Games

Alliances for Every Day

This has little to do with *panem et circenses* but with the everyday challenge: Which wine with which sandwich?

You have probably experienced the simple, but comforting, impact of crusty bread and a delicious wine during a wine tasting. Bread is almost always on the table, and eventually you can't hold yourself back any longer and end up grabbing a piece. Each wine tastes good by itself, but teamed up, this combination is unbeatable. There are countless types of bread, but no matter which you choose, a delicious interaction with wine is the result almost every time.

Experiment:
Three baguettes, each with a different topping, meet three everyday wines. Which bread goes well with which wine, and why?

Note:
It doesn't take much to make good bread: flour, water, salt, and, above all, time to rise, so that the yeast or the leavening can do its work. Due to its crunchy crust, bread has roasted aromas and–depending on the type of flour–a light- or dark-colored, moist-to-savory interior. Furthermore, it contains carbohydrates and starch which, in combination with saliva, give rise to a delayed taste of sweetness. This can have a neutralizing-to-stimulating effect on the acidity, tannins and alcohol content of a wine. With all its ingredients, bread buffers any overly intense wine flavors, while its salt content acts as an additional catalyst and has a pleasant flavor-enhancing effect. Conclusion: bread and wine complement each other perfectly.

Wine Pairing:

For the right wine partnership, you should be aware of this interaction. Using this knowledge, the different toppings and their impact on the taste of wine will be examined.

Matter of Taste:

What is a slice of bread without a topping? The tasteful solidarity ends here, because a different type of wine will be required depending on what tops the bread. A baguette will be topped with everyday foods. For this experiment, however, butter will be avoided to prevent the additional fat element from manipulating the influencing parameters of the topping.

	Goat Cheese — approx. 22 percent fat content, typical chalky texture, and tart taste that coats the palate	Smoked Salmon — approx. 19 percent fat content, salt, smoky notes, soft, rich, palate-coating structure, pleasantly fishy	Salami — approx. 35 percent fat content, spicy, very high salt content, a flavor-enhancing effect
White Wine Type ♀ Riesling — fresh, fruity, animating acidity	☺ The Riesling's fruit sweetness and acidity accompany the chalky goat cheese perfectly.	☹ Fish fat and acidity clash. The Riesling develops an aggressive acidity and a sweet-sour after-taste. Unharmonious metallic mouth-feel.	☹ The salami's high fat content destroys the delicate Riesling's fine, fruity aromas.
White Wine Type ♀♀♀♀ Chardonnay Barrique — powerful, luscious, round, moderate acidity	☹ The tart cheese clashes with alcohol and tannins. The wine becomes bitter and seems more powerful.	☺ The luscious wine encounters smoky notes and richness. The moderate acidity gets boosted, which lifts the fruit aromas and generates a long finish.	☹ Although this white wine has power and alcohol, it has no chance against the salami. It develops a one-dimensional, sweet taste. Red wine tannins are missing.
Red Wine Type 2 ♀♀ Red Wine Cuvée — fruity, youthful acidity, tannins	☹ The red wine's tannins clash with the milk protein and the chalky, tart cheese.	☹ Protein and palate-coating fish fat clash with the red wine's tannins. It develops an astringent, bitter taste.	☺ The fat and the corresponding salt content optimally absorb the red wine tannins, and give the fruity aromas free reign.

Goat Cheese

A young goat cheese (approx. 22 percent fat) with a solid core is our first choice of topping. The young goat cheese is characterized by a subtle, nutty, chalky, tangy taste. Cheese and wine are commonly considered to be ideal partners. Yet the question "Which wine with which cheese?" remains unanswered.

White Wine Type 1

The lively Riesling is immediately monopolized by the goat cheese, and shows its quaffable side. This fresh, fruity drop supports the goat cheese's slightly tangy, somewhat chalky taste. The protein structure of the young goat cheese does not hold up against the alcohol-rich, tannic wines. The acidic flavors combine perfectly with fruity wine flavors, complementing and supporting each other.

White Wine Type 4

The powerful, barrique-aged white wine develops unpleasant bitter notes in combination with the cheese, loses its fruit expression and, thus, its charm. The interaction between the wine's astringent, tannic structure and the milky, slightly sour-tasting, cheese flavor causes the wine to taste bitter. In this combination, the cheese also suffers, making it seem much fattier. It feels almost like a rich crème fraîche, not like a delicate, stimulating goat cheese.

Red Wine Type 2

At first, the red wine takes you off-guard with stimulating red fruit-flavors, but after prolonged contact with the slightly sour goat cheese, it develops persistent bitter notes. In this combination, the wine loses its substance, and seems downright thin and tired, due to the fact that the red wine-tannins do not tolerate the milk protein. This provides clear proof that red wine and fresh goat cheese are not good partners.

Smoked Salmon

We serve a smoked, salted salmon with approx. 19 percent fat, sliced. It's been a long time since salmon was considered a luxury product. Today, it is available in different quality levels, from discount offerings to fine delicatessen selections. A fresh, crusty baguette topped with high-quality, delicately smoked salmon remains one of life's true culinary pleasures. Salmon coats the palate with a soft, rich, mouth-filling sensation, and seduces the senses with salty, smoky or spicy notes, depending on the preparation method of the salmon.

White Wine Type 1

The freshly fruity wine with a marked acidity does not have much to offer in reply to the fat salmon. The fruit flavors are lost, the wine develops metallic notes, and an unpleasant one-dimensional, sweet-sour aftertaste remains.

White Wine Type 4

The smoked salmon has a truly catalytic effect on the wine. The alcohol, mixed with the soft, creamy taste of this barrel-aged wine, bonds with the salmon fat, which allows the fruit flavors to manifest themselves favorably. The wine's roasted flavors are practically leveled by the salmon's smoky notes. This is perfect, because vibrant fruit and freshness remain.

Red Wine Type 2

Although the young red wine has—just like the barrique-aged white wine—roasted flavors, it can't handle the smoked salmon at all. Its tannins cannot deal with the high protein content of the rich fish. The fruit disappears completely, tarry flavors dominate, and the wine appears bitter, metallic and astringent.

Salami

The following experiment is based on the fabulous alliance between the strong-tasting, quite fatty and salty salami (about 35 percent fat); the fresh baguette; and the matching wine. First, taste the salami on its own, without bread, in order to determine its fresh taste; this is perceived only at the very end, after swallowing. It is the high salt content which has a stimulating and flavor-enhancing impact. Your mouth will, literally, start watering.

White Wine Type 1

The freshly fruity wine reacts promptly with discontent, and tingles on the tongue. The wine loses its fruit flavor when put in combination with the salami–it tastes sour, and its finish seems bitter. The salami pushes the delicate, fruity wine to the side and gives it no chance.

White Wine Type 4

The powerful, barrique-aged white wine shows at least a tiny bit of its fruitiness which is abruptly replaced by a distinct sweetness. Alcohol comes to the fore, gives a rustic, slightly sweet taste, and paralyzes the wine's initial brilliance. The fruit flavors are lost.

Red Wine Type 2

The red wine, by contrast, manages wonderfully with the salami. The wine's delicate, spicy notes and tannins absorb the salami's fat and salt, and the fruit aromas are able to come to the fore. The red wine tannins are perfectly buffered by the fat.

The Impact of Sauce
A Formative Taste Element

What would pasta be without sauce? A Sunday roast without gravy? Indeed, quite a dry, rather tasteless matter. The sauce gives these dishes flavor. It is consumed with every bite and, on the palate, it accomplishes the task of bringing all of the ingredients together. Alongside different cooking methods and intensely flavorful herbs and spices, sauces are the undisputed center of a dish. In most cases, they also determine the appropriate wine choice.

It all depends on the sauce. That is why this experiment focuses on the most important combination rules with respect to sauce and wine. In this chapter, we will again use the three wine prototypes from the previous chapter. A good sauce–like a good wine–possesses a multifaceted character. A sauce is, in most cases, predominantly made of fat. Fat, regardless whether it is oil, cream, butter or lard, carries the aroma in the sauce. Therefore, fat behaves in a similar way as alcohol does in wine. Salt has a flavor-enhancing effect, especially in connection with acidity. This is added to the sauce, together with wine and lemon juice or vinegar. Without acidity, a sauce is unstructured, broad and dull.

> A good sauce–like a good wine–
> possesses a multifaceted character.

For an appropriate wine partnership, it is first important to be familiar with the sauce's distinctive aromas and intensities. Is a sauce distinguished by fat, or rather by the acidity or roasted aromas? Does it leave a mouth-filling or a stimulating fresh impression? Is it piquant, or even spicy-hot? Which spices can you taste? And what does this mean for the choice of wine?

	Vinaigrette cold base-sauce with acidity, salt and fat	Beurre blanc warm, white base-sauce with acidity, salt and high fat-content	Jus warm, meat-based, base-sauce with acidity, salt and bitter-tasting roasted flavors	Chutney cold, piquant, slightly sweet, somewhat jammy, spicy sauce	Chili sauce cold, hot-spicy, fruity, slightly sweet-tasting sauce
White Wine Type 1 Riesling fresh, fruity, animating acidity	☹ The acidity increases unpleasantly, and covers up fruit flavors.	☹ Fat and acidity collide. The Riesling develops an aggressive acidity and appears metallic, dull and bitter.	☹ The wine tastes sweet, develops acidic and bitter notes. The roasted flavors destroy the delicately fruity Riesling notes.	☺ In connection with fruit and piquant spice, the Riesling reveals delicious fruit flavors and a creamy texture.	😐 Hot spice gets along wonderfully with the Riesling's sweetness and fruit. The spicier the sauce, the sweeter the wine should be.
White Wine Type 4 Chardonnay Barrique powerful, luscious, round, moderate acidity	😐 The vinaigrette supports the fruit flavors, the wine develops a stimulating acidity and length.	☺ The creamy wine absorbs the buttery sauce. The moderate acidity is increased, which lifts the fruit flavors and creates a long finish.	☹ The slightly bitter jus ruins the wine's creaminess and increases the alcohol perception. Bitter grapefruit notes and a peppery spicy edge.	☹ The fruit flavors vanish completely. The wine appears soft, broad, caramel-like and boring.	☹ The hot spiciness brings bitterness, astringency and alcohol unpleasantly to the fore.
Red Wine Type 2 Red Wine Cuvée fruity, youthful acidity, tannins	☹ Tannins collide with the acidity, fruit vanishes, rough astringency, extreme bitter taste.	☹ The wine absorbs the fat content in this sauce, but it loses its fruit and elegance. Tannins are emphasized, a rough sensation remains on the tongue.	☺ The wine's tannins have a parallel in the lightly bitter roasted flavors found in the jus. Pleasant fruit, stimulating acidity and juicy length.	☹ The wine loses fruit and elegance, appears earthy and bitter. The tannins collide with the sweet-tasting spiciness.	☹ The fruit vanishes, the wine seems almost watery. The wine's bitter tannins collide with the hot spice.

Ready-made or homemade? We've used homemade sauces in our experiment. Though most of the effects can also be achieved with widely available ready-made products, their harmony is usually not quite as fine, because they lack the fresh, high-quality ingredients such as olive oil, vinegar, stock, fresh herbs and spices. Ready-made sauces are usually higher in sugar and acid content, which intensifies negative taste-impressions.

Vinaigrette

This vinaigrette is based on simple high-quality ingredients. Mix mustard, vinegar, honey and veal stock together. Stir in the oils, salt and pepper to taste.

White Wine Type 1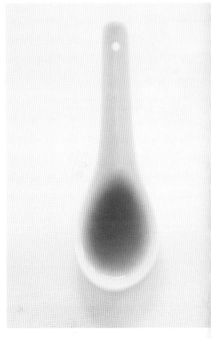

Riesling changes when combined with the vinaigrette. The wine's acidity comes distinctly to the fore, and the Riesling develops unpleasant, exaggerated citrusy aromas. Conclusion: Riesling reacts "sourly" and loses its quaffable fruit.

White Wine Type 4

This opulent Chardonnay gets on quite well with the tangy vinaigrette. The fruit comes to the fore, and the tannins step into the background. Some bitter grapefruit aromas remain. Then a refreshing acidity follows, which is further supported by the vinaigrette, which lends the wine a welcome elegance. The combination of delicate acidity, fruit, and excellently integrated alcohol, contributes to the wine's flattering length.

Red Wine Type 2

In combination with the vinaigrette, the wine's tannins are emphasized in a rather rustic way, and block the taste buds. The fruit recedes, and an unpleasant astringency and an extreme bitter tastes permeates the palate. The wine seems metallic and tastes downright dull; it appears broad and rustic. One gets a similar impression in the mouth as when eating artichokes with a much-too-acidic vinaigrette.

1 ½ tbsp mustard, medium-hot

100 ml Aceto balsamico, white

1 ½ tbsp honey

200 ml veal stock

300 ml canola oil

100 ml olive oil

Salt, pepper

500 g shallots

2 tbsp vegetable oil

8 cl Noilly Prat

1 L dry white wine (preferably Riesling)

2 L fish stock

15 coarsely crushed peppercorns

1 bay leaf

2 twigs of thyme

600 ml heavy cream

10 g starch

400 g ice-cold butter in small
cubes

1 lemon

Salt, pepper

Beurre blanc

Clean and peel shallots, slice into rings, and lightly sauté until soft and translucent. Deglaze the onions with Noilly Prat and Riesling, then fill up with
fish stock. Add the spices and herbs, and reduce the liquid by half. Next, add
heavy cream and reduce again.

Strain the sauce through a fine sieve, and thicken lightly with starch.
Following this, beat in cold cubes of butter with an immersion blender. Add
lemon juice, salt and pepper to taste.

White Wine Type 1 🍷

The Riesling develops an aggressive acidity and appears quite metallic in
combination with the rich, creamy beurre blanc. The sauce's high fat content covers up the fruit, and the Riesling tastes dull, bitter and simply sour.

White Wine Type 4 🍷🍷🍷🍷

The Chardonnay shows off its opulence with tongue-caressing creaminess
and a luscious fruit explosion. With its rich structure, it completely absorbs
the fat content of the buttery sauce. Delicate, stimulating grapefruit aromas
lend lively freshness and a pleasant complexity to this combination. The
wine's moderate acidity is refreshingly intensified, and with this acidity the
fruit aromas come to the fore, and remain on the palate longer.

Red Wine Type 2 🍷🍷

Tannins are emphasized and create an unpleasantly rough sensation on the
tongue. The fruit withdraws into the background. Although the wine begins
by absorbing the fat content, it loses its stimulating fruit aromas and its elegance during the process. What remains is something earthy and bitter. This
combination doesn't deliver any pleasure.

Jus

Roast the bones in a deep casserole dish, and place in a 230 degree-Celsius oven. Add the diced root vegetables, and continue roasting in oil with the bones, until they begin to brown. Add the leek later because it can burn easily, creating a bitter taste. Add tomato paste, roast everything together, turn the bones and deglaze with red wine. Continue to roast it all, reduce and deglaze again. This way, the sauce's intensity and color can be influenced. The longer the ingredients roast, the darker the sauce will get. At the very end, fill the dish with veal stock, add spices and herbs, and reduce down for one hour. Strain the sauce through a rough cloth and cook down again. The sauce will have reached the desired consistency once it has reduced down to one-third of its original amount.

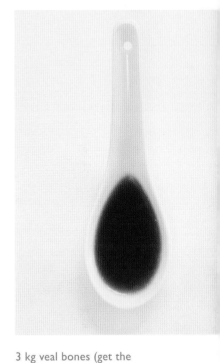

White Wine Type I

The Riesling tastes slightly sweet at first, then citrus aromas and a persistent bitter taste follow. The Riesling's fresh fruit-taste vanishes completely. The roasted aromas of the jus destroy the delicately fruity character of this light wine.

White Wine Type 4

Tart grapefruit notes dominate with an unpleasant bitter taste. This is accompanied by a persistent, almost peppery abrasiveness. The wine falls apart and becomes spirituous. The rich jus—with its powerful meaty taste, and its roasted flavors—destroys the Chardonnay's fruit and creaminess.

Red Wine Type 2

The sauce acts almost as a catalyst and intensifies the wine's aromas. The fruit notes appear youthfully fresh, with juiciness, magnificent length and potential. The red wine's tannins find their parallel in the jus' slightly bitter, roasted aromas.

Tip: pour the jus in an ice cube tray, and freeze. This way, there is always a concentrated base-sauce on-hand with which to cook. Should one want to change the jus' consistency, it can be thickened with starch and butter.

3 kg veal bones (get the butcher to chop them into small pieces)
500 g root vegetables (celery, onions, carrots, parsley root and leek)
2 tbsp vegetable oil
2 tbsp tomato paste
700 ml full-bodied red wine
2 L veal stock
I sprig rosemary
I sprig marjoram
2 bay leaves
2 cloves
2 garlic cloves
Salt, pepper

Chutney

Clean pears and bell peppers carefully, remove all seeds, and peel the peppers. Dice both into 0.5 cm cubes and simmer together with the remaining 10 ingredients for 10 minutes, stirring constantly. Reduce the temperature and cook down to a thick mass. Remove the spices after two hours, and pour the chutney into small jars. When poured into jars at a minimum temperature of 80 degrees Celsius and sealed in an airtight container, it can be stored for up to three months.

White Wine Type 1

The yellow bell pepper's taste melds wonderfully with the fresh pear. The chutney possesses a high fruit and vegetable content, and a piquant spiciness. With this, it easily incorporates the Riesling's fruit sweetness and highlights its lively texture. This combination whets your appetite. Beware of store-bought chutney, which often contains too much sweetness, which can encumber the Riesling.

White Wine Type 4

The creamy Chardonnay has great difficulties with the chutney. The wine appears soft, broad, caramelized and boring. The fruit aromas vanish completely, the wine becomes thin and almost bitter, and seems overly oaky and awkward. The Chardonnay cannot deal with the chutney's piquant spiciness and sweet fruit characteristics. A cream-based fat element—or at least a buffering side dish—is missing. The wine reacts literally with "embitterment."

Red Wine Type 2

The wine's fruit is only briefly apparent, but it then loses its elegance and its stimulating fruit aromas, and appears earthy, bitter and almost unpalatable. The tannins collide with the chutney's sweet, fruit aromas and piquant spiciness.

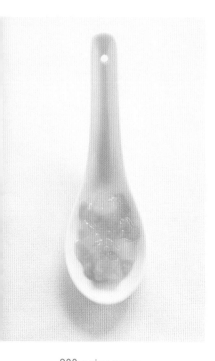

900 g ripe pears

900 g yellow bell peppers

100 g sugar

1 cinnamon stick

1 clove

1 bay leaf

1/2 star anise

90 ml Aceto balsamico, white

200 g jam sugar

30 g salt

Chili Sauce

Peel and clean the shallots and chili peppers, then peel the garlic cloves and mince and lightly brown everything in canola oil. Deglaze with orange juice and veal stock.

Add the white balsamic vinegar and honey, then reduce. Season to taste with salt, pepper and sugar. This sauce can be kept in a cool place for up to four weeks if it has been poured into jars and tightly sealed right after preparation.

White Wine Type 1

Normally, fruity, sweet Riesling basks in this combination. Unfortunately, our prototype's sweetness level isn't quite high enough. The hot spice takes away a bit of the wine's fruit. It's unbearable to imagine how perfectly a Riesling with a higher residual sweetness would nestle up against this sauce: hot spice gets along beautifully with sweetness. The lively, fruity acidity is a refreshing counterbalance.

White Wine Type 4

The Chardonnay develops a bitter flavor. The tannin frame—which comes from barrel-aging—the creaminess, and the alcohol collide with the hot spiciness in the sauce. The alcohol, and an aggravating bitterness in the form of acerbic grapefruit aromas, are emphasized. On the palate, the sauce's hot spice gets left behind, along with these unattractive, bitter notes. This sauce destroys the character of the wine.

Red Wine Type 2

Except for some light raspberry notes, the fruit vanishes completely. The wine seems almost watery. Also, the wine's tannins collide with the hot spice of the sauce, which destroys the wine's remaining attributes, such as fruit and juiciness, and leaves behind a desolate trail of bitterness.

1 tbsp shallots

1 tbsp fresh chilis

2 garlic cloves

1 tbsp canola oil

200 ml orange juice

300 ml veal stock

30 ml Aceto balsamico, white

100 g honey

Salt, pepper

Sugar

CULINARY EXPERIMENT

Nº 3

Harmony and Conflict

Birds of a Feather Flock Together—Opposites Attract

In this chapter, two experiments are combined. The first part describes a combination in which harmony is achieved with the help of matching flavors, and in the second part tension is caused by using contrasting flavors.

The idea behind this culinary experiment is to use the same product processed in two different ways. For this, the fish or meat will be individually prepared, and then paired with varietal wines of various styles. For example, pike perch will be paired with different Pinot Blanc wines while the pork dish will be matched with different Pinot Noir styles. How does this affect these particular combinations? What happens when, and why?

Instructions:

You should plan to set some time aside for this experiment, because preparing and cooking all three dishes is an elaborate task. Before you try the different dishes, you should first taste the wines. Then, try each dish with each of the three wines. Find out which wine forms the best alliance with which dish.

Harmony via matching aromas:
Pike perch and Pinot Blanc

Harmony via differing aromas:
Pork and Pinot Noir

Result:

The differences are relatively clear. Since the cooking methods and ingredients vary for each dish, different facets emerge from the combinations with each accompanying wine.

Balanced Alliances: Harmony

When you start to pair food and wine, you first look for partners whose tastes go well together. Since it is much easier to search for similar tastes, these three pike-perch recipes are good lessons for beginners.

Experiment:
Three different-tasting pike-perch dishes take on three distinct types of Pinot Blanc.

Experiment	Harmony via unifying aromas Pike Perch & Pinot Blanc	
	Pike Perch vegetal, fresh, light	**White Wine Type 1** Pinot Blanc light and fresh
	Pike Perch rich, creamy, aromatic	**White Wine Type 3** Pinot Blanc complex and elegant
	Pike Perch rich, creamy, roasted	**White Wine Type 4** Pinot Blanc powerful and opulent

Notes:
The basic component of this experiment, pike perch, is constant. Changes are made only to the method of preparation, as well as to the side dishes, but, as a consequence, the overall taste impression of the dish changes. Three different specifications are required for the different types of Pinot Blanc. To achieve a harmonious interaction, the type of preparation (e.g., grilled, fried or poached); the intensity of the spices; and, of course, the linking sauce, take center stage.

Wine Pairing:
The Pinot Blanc grape variety has been chosen as the suitable wine accompaniment. Just like the pike perch dish, wines of this variety are, of course, available in different characteristic styles. In this case, they come from different growing regions with unique soils, and all show the personal touch of the winemaker. One comes in the form of a light, fresh drop; the next one as a Grosses Gewächs or Grand Cru with an elegant creaminess; and another in the form of a more opulent, oak-aged treasure. These are common wine types

with different characteristics and quality levels. You could perform this experiment using Chardonnay or Pinot Gris, if they meet the established taste-parameters of our wine type examples.

A Matter of Taste:

Vegetables, pasta, cream and roasted aromas encounter the fruity, creamy and exciting Pinot Blanc. What does this mean in practice?

	Poached Pike Perch on Spring Vegetables	Fried Pike Perch with Lobster Sauce and Parsley Pasta	Fried Pike Perch Wrapped in Bacon on Lentils with Pinot Blanc Sauce
White Wine Type 1 2011 Weißburgunder (Pinot Blanc) Stephan Steinmetz, Mosel, Germany	🙂 The fish behaves neutrally. The vegetables buffer the acidity and highlight the Pinot Blanc's fruit and delicate creaminess.	🙁 The Pinot Blanc is too light for this alliance. It reacts with unpleasant acidity and muted fruit expression.	🙁 The bacon's roasted notes pose a challenge for the wine, as does the rich sauce. The wine reacts with muted fruit and an almost aggressive acidity.
White Wine Type 3 2009 Mandelberg Weißburgunder (Pinot Blanc) Großes Gewächs, Dr. Wehrheim, Pfalz, Germany	🙁 The dish is too light for this complex wine, which doesn't bond well with the vegetable aromas. Due to this, it bluntly reacts in an acidic and almost bitter way.	🙂 The pasta buffers the youthful acidity. Delicate, roasted notes and creamy lobster aromas cling softly to this smooth, and pleasantly drinkable, complex wine.	🙁 This dish goes over the top with respect to the wine. Clearly too extreme in roasted notes for the wine's rather elegant, fruity smoothness, it reacts with muted fruit, acidity and harsh notes.
White Wine Type 4 2011 Weißburgunder "C" (Pinot Blanc) Schneider, Endingen, Baden, Germany	🙁 The dish is too light for this opulent wine type. The lack of richness emphasizes the wine's alcohol and barrique notes.	🙁 Roasted aromas and cream sauce are definitely better partners than vegetables and vinaigrette. But there still isn't a flavor equivalent for the opulent fruit aromas and oaky notes.	🙂 The creamed lentils with root vegetables and fried bacon are (positively) challenging. The opulent wine type clings to these flavors, showing off its opulent fruit and smooth richness.

Poached Pike Perch
With Spring Vegetables
Vegetal, Fresh and Light

1 shallot
100 g celery root
100 g leek
2 sprigs of parsley
50 ml white wine (Pinot Blanc)
2 tsp salt
4 pike perch fillets (160 g each)
Spring vegetables:
100 g green beans
100 g flat beans
100 g carrots
500 g green asparagus
Salt
1 leek
20 g butter
Pepper
Freshly ground nutmeg
1/2 bunch parsley (chopped)

For the stock, mince the shallot, celery root, leek and parsley. Add this to a pot filled with the wine, 500 ml water, and two tablespoons of salt, bring to a boil and simmer for 15 minutes. Put the pike perch fillets in the gently simmering stock, so that they are completely submerged. Then, cook for five minutes at 90 degrees Celsius with the skin-side up.

Slice the green beans, flat beans and carrots into two cm pieces. Peel the lower third of the green asparagus, cut off the dry ends, and then slice at an angle into 2 cm pieces. Parboil the vegetables separately in boiling salt-water for about two minutes, then rinse with ice-cold water and drip-dry.

Shortly before serving, slice the remaining leek into thin rings. Melt butter in a pan, and sauté the leek for about one minute. Then, add the parboiled vegetables to the pan and season to taste with salt, pepper and a dash of nutmeg. Sprinkle with chopped parsley before serving.

White Wine Type 1 🍷
Light and Fresh

What Happens?

This light, fresh springtime dish that thrives on the subtle, nuanced flavors of the poached pike perch, fresh herbs and crisp vegetables. Pike perch is a predatory fish that lives in rivers, where it is very active and swims quickly. Its flesh is very muscular and stays firm, even after it is cooked. Beans and asparagus are normally neutral, and have more of a supportive effect on young, dry, fresh and fruity wines. They enhance the wine's aromas, and stabilize its acidity. So they are undoubtedly one of the bridge-builders for successful wine and food pairing. Root vegetables, in turn, are especially important for wines with pronounced acidity; their higher starch content acts as an excellent buffer. The butter connects the individual ingredients; acidity provides freshness and balance; and sea salt enhances the taste.

Result:

The light Pinot Blanc is at ease in this partnership, and its animated fruit aromas, smoky minerality, and soft creaminess can unfold. A fat-laden sauce would most likely overwhelm this light wine. It would have to struggle with the fat content, and would go sour as a result.

**2011 Weißburgunder (Pinot Blanc)
Stephan Steinmetz, Mosel, Germany**

This lively Pinot Blanc has a pale, yellow color with green tinges. It smells enticingly of pear and lemon, but is also a touch smoky and minerally, influenced by the chalky soil in which the vines are planted. Despite this wine's fresh and stimulating lightness, its scent immediately lures you with substance and succulence; the first signs of quality. The first impression it makes on the palate is not disappointing. This organically produced wine spends its first months in stainless steel, and captivates with its pure and clean style; zesty juiciness; and delicious, soft viscosity. The vivid, well-integrated acidity gives the wine its necessary backbone, and guarantees a long finish. With an alcohol content of 11.5 percent by volume, this is a lightweight wine, but with great depth-of-flavors.

Pan-fried Pike Perch with Lobster Sauce and Parsley Pasta
Rich, Creamy and Aromatic

4 pike perch filets (160 g each)
Salt and white pepper
Flour for dusting
2 tbsp olive oil
1 sprig of thyme
2 tbsp butter
400 g flat-ribbon pasta (Tagliatelle)
1 bunch Italian parsley
250 ml lobster stock
50 ml heavy cream
1 tsp starch
Salt, pepper
White wine (Pinot Blanc)
1 dash Noilly Prat
Lemon juice
80 g cold butter

Season the pike-perch fillets with salt and pepper, and lightly dust the skin-side with flour. Heat olive oil in an oven-proof pan, then add the thyme sprig. First, fry the fish fillets skin-side down until they are golden yellow, then turn over. Add the butter, allow it to froth up, and then cook everything in a 160 degree-Celsius-oven for about three minutes.

Cook the pasta al dente, drain, and mix with finely chopped parsley. For the lobster sauce, bring the lobster stock, together with the cream, to a boil and reduce. Stir one tablespoon of starch in cold water until smooth, and thicken the sauce. Season with salt, pepper, white wine, Noilly Prat and a dash or two of freshly squeezed lemon juice. Take the sauce from the stove, and gradually whisk in the ice-cold butter.

White Wine Type 3 🍷🍷🍷
Complex and Elegant

What Happens?

It is clear that the sauce plays the leading role in this dish. To make the stock used in the sauce, lobster carcasses are roasted with root vegetables, deglazed, and then reduced. The added tomato paste enhances the slightly bitter, roasted flavors. To extract sufficient flavor and color from the carcasses, they are subsequently flambéed with brandy. The finished sauce has an intensely strong lobster taste. Pasta contains starch in the form of carbohydrates, which buffers all kinds of acid. Hence, both salt and acid are important when generating the necessary tension between the individual ingredients. With pasta, this effect is best achieved with a fresh, lively, intensely flavored sauce.

Result:

The smoky notes of the crustacean sauce bond perfectly with the Pinot Blanc's complex flavors, while the pasta effortlessly buffers the youthful acidity. This profound wine can easily handle the sauce's fat content, as well as the gently fried pike perch's roasted flavors.

2009 Mandelberg Weißburgunder GG (Pinot Blanc) Dr. Wehrheim, Pfalz, Germany

This complex Pinot Blanc at first presents only smoky mineral notes; not until it is sufficiently exposed to oxygen does it show its true flavor spectrum: yellow fruits, ripe pear and tart apple peel. The linear minerality

defines a still-dormant potential, which is confirmed later on the palate. The juicy, well-integrated acidity carries the complex fruit flavors and leads to a refreshing, delicate bitterness that gives the wine backbone and character. This full-bodied Pinot Blanc has never seen the inside of a barrel. But it has a substance which is rich in extract.

Fried Pike Perch Wrapped in Bacon on Lentils in Pinot Blanc Sauce
Rich, Creamy and Roasted

4 pike perch filets (160 g each)
8 thin slices of bacon
1 sprig thyme
Oil for frying
2 shallots (diced)
2 tbsp olive oil
150 g Puy lentils
50 g yellow lentils
4 tbsp Champagne vinegar
250 ml vegetable broth
1 bay leaf
1 sprig thyme
1 sprig rosemary
1 carrot
1/2 leek
salt and pepper
10 g sugar
20 g butter
100 ml veal jus
3 sprigs of Italian parsley
2 shallots (diced)
100 g butter, of which 50 g should be ice-cold to bind the sauce
200 ml Pinot Blanc
100 ml fish stock
100 ml heavy cream
Salt

Wrap each fish fillet with two thin bacon slices. Distribute the thyme leaves across the fillets and press them on the skin lightly. First, fry the fillets skin-side down, so the bacon gets crispy, but doesn't fall apart. After this, cook for about three minutes in a pre-heated 160 degree-Celsius-oven.

Sauté the diced shallots in olive oil. Add the pre-soaked lentils and sauté them while stirring. Deglaze with vinegar and fill up with broth. Add the herbs, and cook until the lentils are done. Finely chop the carrot and the leek. Add the vegetables to the lentils when one minute of cooking time remains. Season to taste with salt, pepper and sugar. Add butter and veal jus at the end. Shortly before serving, fold in the chopped parsley.

For the sauce: sauté diced shallots in 50 g of butter. Deglaze with Pinot Blanc, add fish stock, and bring it all to a boil, then reduce the sauce to one-third. Fill up with heavy cream, and bind with the remaining ice-cold butter. Season with salt to taste.

White Wine Type 4 ♥♥♥♥
Powerful and Opulent

What Happens?

This wine's pronounced tannins and roasted aromas stem from oak-barrel-aging, and it can, therefore, tolerate some rich resistance. The slightly earthy and sweet-tasting lentils with root vegetables, thyme, and rosemary aromas buffer the youthful and zesty characteristics of this powerful wine. In addition, the crispy-fried bacon offers up another flavor connection to this compact, tannic wine. But this combination obtains the ultimate kick from the rich, white wine-sauce which is made with plenty of cream and butter, therefore enabling it to really cling to its wine partner.

**2011 Weißburgunder "C"
(Pinot Blanc)
Schneider,
Baden, Germany**

This powerful Pinot Blanc emerges as very expressive on the nose, with delicate vanilla notes, yellow fruits, pear, yellow plum, some grapefruit and a hint of wood. Only when the wine has had some time to breathe

Result:

This dish is the perfect partner for a creamy, barrel-aged white wine—the bitter tannins are perfectly buffered, and the fruity notes are able to take over. This combination offers advantages for both sides—this particularly powerful dish also reaps benefits by having found a lively, complementary partner in this wine.

will its power and structure become noticeable. The acidity provides necessary balance. It supports both the ripe fruit flavors as well as fruity, bitter grapefruit notes, and brings them to the fore. These tangy, fruity, phenolic notes are, in the truest sense of the word, bitterly needed. They have a supportive effect, lend structure, and give this rich Pinot Blanc its requisite elegance. The alcohol is very well-integrated. The tannins are superbly buffered by the creamy richness and provide an intense, fruity finish.

Conflicting Alliances: Contrast

The following experiment is a step up in difficulty from the last one, for all those people who have cooked, tested and tasted their way through the standard knowledge of combination techniques. Now similar and harmonious flavors won't be sought; instead tension will be created between contrasting aromas.

Experiment:

Three differently prepared loins of pork come up against three distinct types of Pinot Noir.

Experiment	Harmony via contrasting aromas Pork and Pinot Noir	
	Pork refreshing, fruity, meaty	**Red Wine Type 2** 🍷 Pinot Noir youthful, fruity and harmonious
	Pork piquant, citrusy, aromatic	**Red Wine Type 3** 🍷🍷🍷 Pinot Noir complex and elegant
	Pork rich, fatty-sweet, acidic	**Red Wine Type 3** 🍷🍷🍷 Pinot Noir elegant and mature

Notes:

Savory spices, such as pepper, can detrimentally affect a red wine's fruitiness, or even clash with its tannins. An overly high fat content, when it isn't buffered, can possibly have difficulties with a wine's expressive acidity. And in some cases, acidity can become amplified–an expressive acidity in wine isn't necessarily compatible with the acidity in food. But there are other ways to make wine and food work together.

Wine Pairing:

In this case a grape variety plays a leading role: Pinot Noir, first in a light village-style; then as a complex, profound top growth; and, finally, as a mature, elegant Burgundy. A well-conceived combination of ingredients makes the difference in this experiment. Prerequisites include product knowledge, gustatory memory, and an extensive wealth of experience about how certain ingredients react with each other. Aromatic and acidic wines can bring a delicious vitality to the marriage of wine and food; animate the palate; provide flavor tension; as well as whet the appetite for the next bite.

A Matter of Taste:

Fruit aromas, acidity and sweetness come up against red wine-tannins. What does this mean in practice? Pork with or without the bone, roasted, spiced, aromatized, peppered, with or without sweetness, buffering vegetables or noodles, but always with a hint of acidity. What are the results when combining these variations with different types of Pinot Noir? What factors are important for lean, elegant or even mature types? Find the right type for each dish.

	Pork Cutlet With Glazed Loquats, Green Asparagus, Chanterelles and Celery Purée	Pork Loin With Honey, Pepper and Lemon-Zest Glaze, Cauliflower Risotto and Leeks	Pork Cutlet With Caramalized Onion-Crust, Spaetzle and Parsley Salad
Red Wine Type 1 🍷 2006 Pinot Noir Village, Jürgen von der Mark, Baden, Germany	🙂 Loquats and asparagus lend freshness and highlight the wine's fruit aromas, while the acidity is buffered by the roasted fat rind. The lean Pinot Noir is a friendly partner.	☹ The wine is too light for the alliance with the caramelized pepper crust. It reacts with the food's sweetness with provocative acidity.	☹ The onion crust appears rich, almost sweet, the parsley salad is vegetal. The wine reacts with a sour impression; it loses structure.
Red Wine Type 3 🍷🍷🍷 2009 Pinot Noir, Eichholz, Irene Grünenfelder, Graubünden, Switzerland	😐 The dish is too fresh and fruity, all-in-all too light for the complex wine. The acidity is emphasized and the tannins come to the fore.	🙂 The caramelized pepper crust and the lemon zest unite salt, sweetness and acid in a stimulating, lightly bitter affair. The Pinot Noir's fruity aromas and juicy richness come to the fore.	☹ The rich onion crust needs more contrastive flavors. The parsley salad brings about green notes, which unpleasantly highlight the wine's acidity and the youthful tannins of this still-restrained Pinot Noir.
Red Wine Type 3 🍷🍷🍷 1994 Chambolle Musigny Les Amoureuses, 1er Cru, Comte de Vogüe, Burgundy, France	😐 The loquats' acidity emphasizes the mature aromas in an unpleasant way. They appear green, and the wine loses its complexity and becomes thin.	😐 The mature aromas of this 1er Cru have to struggle with the caramelized, sweet-pepper crust. The food is too intense for this delicate wine, and it reacts with a sour taste.	🙂 The parsley salad emphasizes freshness in this combination, while the rich crust perfectly balances the wine's mature notes.

Pork Cutlet with Loquats, Green Asparagus, Chanterelles and Celery Purée
Refreshing, Fruity and Meaty

500 g celeriac (diced)
Salt
50 ml heavy cream
2 tbsp crème fraîche
80 g butter
Pepper
4 pork cutlets (Duke of Berkshire)
Coarse black pepper
Oil
100 ml sherry
500 ml veal stock
500 g green asparagus
Sugar
4 loquats
300 g chanterelles

Cook diced celeriac in salt water until tender. Strain off water, add heavy cream, crème fraiche and purée. Melt 30 g butter in a pan until foamy and lightly brown, and add to the celeriac mixture. Purée again until smooth. Season to taste with salt and pepper.

Score the fat rind surrounding the cutlet, and season with salt and coarse, black pepper. Slowly brown the cutlet with the fat-side down. Then, brown all sides and finish cooking for approx. 12 minutes in a 160 degree-Celsius pre-heated oven.

Heat sherry in a sauce pan and fill up with the veal stock. Reduce to the desired consistency, and then bind with 30 g ice-cold butter. Glaze the cleaned asparagus in butter with salt and sugar. Cut the cleaned loquats into slices. Sauté the cleaned chanterelles in some oil, season and then add the remaining butter. Add the loquats and briefly sauté together.

Red Wine Type 2 🍷🍷
Fruity and Harmonious

What Happens?

The pork cutlet's thick rind of fat serves to carry the flavor of this otherwise delicate-tasting meat. The rind was scored before browning so that the fat could become crispy, and the desired roasted aromas could develop (Maillard reaction, see page 97). The Pinot Noir reacts in great contrast with the delicious fat rind (comparable to a roast goose–its crispy skin is what's actually pleasing). The jus seems light, but it is rich, fatty and sweet, and creates a connection with the wine's fresh acidity that is perfectly balanced, and unbelievably multifaceted. Now the side dishes will come into play: the creamy, slightly earthy tasting celeriac purée and the sautéed chanterelles have a harmonizing effect on the tannins, while the green asparagus and, most of all, the loquats give not only a refreshing color, but also lend perceptible fruit sweetness and lively acidity.

Result:

With this preparation method, tension is generated by using contrasting components, and that's what gives the flavor kick. The use of acid is well-directed, giving the dish the necessary balance and a pleasant freshness. The fruit acid of the loquats serves to "tip the scales," and acts in conjunction with salt as a flavor-enhancer for the Pinot Noir.

2006 Pinot Noir Village Jürgen von der Mark, Baden, Germany

A light-colored, ruby-red Pinot Noir with expressive, juicy, cherry, delicate oak notes. The aromas are fresh and balanced, and whet the appetite for the first sip. A lively acidity supports the animated fruit notes, and lends the wine lovely vitality and structure. All-in-all, it's an intensely flavored, harmonious Pinot Noir with balance and an appealing finish.

Pork Loin with Honey, Pepper and Lemon-Zest Glaze, Cauliflower-Risotto with Leeks
Piquant, Citrusy-fruity and Aromatic

600 g pork loin, de-boned
(Duke of Berkshire)
150 ml Madeira
500 ml veal stock
20 g cold butter
I leek
Salt
Sugar
250 g cauliflower
I shallot (finely diced)
Olive oil
100 g risotto rice (Carnaroli)
50 ml white wine
300 ml warm stock
50 g Parmesan
2 tbsp whipped cream
2 tbsp honey
2 tbsp coarse black pepper
I tbsp candied lemon zest
(lemon strips which have
been thrice blanched and
candied in sugar syrup)
Coarse sea salt

Cut pork loin in half lengthwise, trim, and wrap—first in plastic wrap, then in aluminum foil. Poach in 80-degree-Celsius water for 20 minutes. Reduce the Madeira by half in a sauce pan, then fill the pan with veal stock. Reduce the sauce to the desired consistency, and then thicken with cold butter.

Slice the green parts of the leek into strips. Glaze the strips in a pan with salt, sugar and some water. Cut the cauliflower into small florets. Sauté the diced shallots in olive oil. Add the rice, season with just a little salt, and add white wine. Stirring constantly, keep adding broth until the rice is cooked, but still firm. Add the cauliflower, and simmer together until the cauliflower is done. Fold in freshly grated parmesan and whipped cream.

Unpack the pork loin, and first fry the fat side. Then, quickly fry on all sides. Caramelize the honey, add coarse pepper and then glaze the meat. Add lemon zest and salt at the very end.

Red Wine Type 3 ♟♟♟
Complex and Elegant

What Happens?

Honey and butter are heated in a pan, slowly caramelized, seasoned with plenty of coarse pepper, with coarse sea salt being added at the end.

The tension in this dish is caused by the lemon zest, which was blanched and candied several times in sugar syrup to tone down the ethereal, bitter notes. Now the tangy, fruity, slightly bitter taste of the lemon zest is emphasized in an extremely stimulating way. Together with the salt, it evens out the sweetness of the caramelized honey. Thus, the fruity-spicy pepper crust creates an appealing tension, because it links all the components together. While the leeks neutralize the effect of the tannins, the cauliflower risotto, which would not necessarily be a classical red wine-partner on its own, is discreetly, but deliciously, emphasized.

Result:

The real decision to be made, however, is the choice between the fine fruit and juicy acidity of the Pinot Noir, and the caramelized pepper-crust with sea salt and the bitter lemon zest. This link challenges and titillates the flavors of the Pinot Noir, targeting the elegance and complexity. Instead of cozy harmony, a delicious tension is created. This is quite possibly a recipe, because of its ingredients, that so many would have, understandably, paired with a more opulent, barrique-aged white wine!

**2009 Pinot Noir Eichholz
Irene Grünenfelder,
Graubünden, Switzerland**

This is a wine with expressive, sour cherry aromas accompanied by spicy, delicately peppery notes and a touch of cedar wood. The lively acidity intertwines with the wine's juicy richness in a focused, almost puristic way. It is accompanied by a delicate minerality and perfectly integrated alcohol.

Due to its youthful state, the finale seems somewhat restrained, and finishes with refreshing acidity, delicious fruit, and a silky texture. This is a complex, multilayered and elegant Pinot Noir with structure, potential and cellar-worthiness.

Pork Cutlet with Caramelized Onion-Crust, Spaetzle and Parsley Salad
Rich, Fat, Sweet and Acidic

5 shallots
60 g butter
4 pork cutlets (Duke of Berkshire)
Salt, coarse black pepper
100 g bread crumbs (from dark rye bread)
100 ml Madeira
600 ml veal stock
20 g cold butter
1 small bunch of parsley
1 shallot
30 g marinated capers
30 ml olive oil
Juice of half a lemon
500 g spaetzle (a Swabian egg noodle specialty)

Dice the shallots finely. Melt 60 g butter (until foamy), add diced shallots and brown lightly. Season the cutlets on all sides with salt and coarse pepper and brown with fat-side down. Then roast on the grill for about 12 minutes in a pre-heated 160-degree-Celsius oven.

Distribute the sautéed, diced shallots onto the cutlets, sprinkle with the bread crumbs, and gratinate briefly under the grill. To make the sauce, reduce the Madeira by one-half with veal stock, and reduce down to the desired consistency. Thicken with cold butter.

Tear the parsley leaves coarsely, slice the shallot into thin rings, and season with capers, olive oil, lemon juice, salt and pepper to taste.

Sauté the cooked spaetzle in butter and distribute onto plates. Add the cutlet, and dress with sauce and parsley salad.

Red Wine Type 3 ♈♈♈
Elegant and Mature

What Happens?

Are you concerned that this mature Pinot Noir will not withstand the parsley salad's acidity and vegetal aromas? Understandable. Typically, boeuf bourguignon would be the likely choice. Capers and lemon juice are included in the parsley salad. They are intensely acidic, and this could definitely harm the wine's balance. With a nearly 20-year-old Burgundy—moreover from a cooler vintage—you would have good reason to be skeptical. In this combination, the meat behaves in a more neutral way and, together with the spaetzle, buffers the parsley salad's acidity with its crust. The crucial point is, and remains, the parsley salad, whose ingredients possess a certain vegetal aggressiveness.

Result:

Parsley and capers contribute lively freshness and, together with salt and lemon juice, have a deliciously stimulating effect on the mature wine. One only has to be careful with the lemon juice, otherwise the acidity can be a touch too aggressive for the wine. Here you can enjoy a dream combination, in which the wine, as well as the food, come perfectly into their own, both spreading their aromas and creating a desire for more!

1994 Chambolle Musigny Les Amoureuses 1er Cru, Comte de Vogüe, Burgundy, France

This mature, ruby-red Burgundy has seductive aromas of ripe, red berries, dried sour cherries, peppery notes, some forest floor with moss and leaves as well as cigar box. A delicious, silky wine, it would benefit from some oxygen to help it to open up fully. The palate is rewarded with a pleasant maturity, an enjoyably lively acidity and unexpected

complexity. Again, aromas of juicy, ripe sour cherries accentuate its taste profile. Due to its multi-layered depth, the oak component and alcohol are hardly detectable, but are part of the very well-matured wine which, next to its structured length, possesses good potential for further development.

Pas de Deux

Truffled Tidbits Meet Mature Bordelaise

In the following experiment, black Périgord truffles are combined with different foods. The intoxicating, earthy aroma is revealed in varying degrees of intensity, depending on the ingredients and method of preparation. Find out why classic Bordeaux wines–from refreshingly young to pleasantly mature–prove to be perfect truffle partners.

It is the irresistible aroma which makes truffles a sought-after delicacy. But even if you get your hands on one of these rare bulbs, it is not automatically guaranteed that it will also excel in taste. In addition to exorbitant prices, varying qualities and tasteless fakes make a connoisseur's life difficult. Moreover, truffles have the characteristic trait of growing some 30 to 50 centimeters below the ground. At this depth they are well-hidden as well as impossible to detect by the human nose. For this reason animal helpers–whose sense of smell is many times finer–are used for the treasure hunt.

Today, however, the invaluable work of a truffle hog is usually carried out by eagerly sniffing dogs.

Contrary to myth, which alleges that the scent of sexual pheromones supposedly contained in truffles sets animals on the track, it is actually the scent of an ordinary sulfur compound, such as the pungently-smelling substance *dimethylsulfide*. This compound contains a molecule which bears a certain resemblance to a boar's sexual hormone; otherwise, the odor is not clearly definable. Truffles don't have an explicit key aroma; in fact, their beguiling scent results from the combination of a variety of aromas. Only in combination do they trigger this earthy, compelling, immensely appealing aroma sensation, which includes other sulfur compounds, alcohols and much more. A truffle's aroma composition can vary depending on its origin and its symbiotic environment. Even slight shifts in concentrations can cause tremendous changes in the fragrance.

Experiment:

In this experiment we will try truffles with crusty bread, tender fish and succulent chicken. All three variations contain a generous dose of fat and salt, but
are prepared in different ways: raw, cooked and fried. What effect do different
foods have on truffles, and on the appropriate wine selection? And what role
does the preparation method and serving temperature play? First, try the
wines. Then, try each dish with each wine to find out what impact truffles
have on Bordeaux wines of different persuasions.

Experiment	How do truffles influence mature red wine? What role do ingredients and method of preparation play?	
	Truffles on Buttered Bread	**Red Wine Type 1** 🍷 Bordeaux, llight and fresh - slightly mature
	Fish with Truffles	**Red Wine Type 2** 🍷🍷 Bordeaux, fruity and harmonious - slightly mature
	Truffled Chicken	**Red Wine Type 2** 🍷🍷 Bordeaux, fruity and harmonious - very mature

Serving Advice:

There are countless philosophies about how truffles should be served. A flavor
carrier in the form of fat or egg yolk is most certainly needed to best release a
truffle's unique aroma. Additionally, the umami contained in truffles provides
a natural flavor-enhancement. In order that the Périgord truffle's irresistible
aroma doesn't quickly evaporate or lose its intensity, truffles should not be
subjected to a long cooking process. Depending on how they will be served,
they can be sliced thinly, cut into fine, julienned strips, or just shaved paper-
thin with a truffle slicer. Because the delicious aroma unfolds more fully with
a slightly increased temperature, the black truffle is usually shaved onto the
warm dish.

Wine Accompaniment:

Which wine goes best with this magic bulb, whose appearance is more reminiscent of a shriveled potato than a black "diamond of the kitchen"? I have
quite deliberately restricted my selection by choosing only red Bordeaux

wines to pair with black Périgord truffles. This experiment could also be easily reproduced with wines from Piedmont or with blends of similar character (e.g., lively acidity and ripe tannins). Dishes made with Périgord truffles are literally predestined for mature Bordeaux because the aged wine's typical leather and forest-floor notes combine perfectly with the earthy truffle aromas.

Matter of Taste:

For this experiment, you will need patience and an extra big-budget. Take your time and cook the individual dishes with quality ingredients. Truffles deserve adequate company. Taste the wines with all three dishes. You will find that each wine will pair with a dish particularly well.

	Truffles on Buttered Bread	Fish with Truffles	Chicken with Truffles
Red Wine Type 1 2006 Château Le Bourdieu, Cru Bourgeois 12.5% Vol.	😊 The light, red wine gains from the earthy truffle aroma and shows lively fruit and delicious length.	☹️ Too light for the pan-fried fish and fennel with red wine truffle-butter. The wine seems one-dimensional and metallic.	☹️ Too light for the truffle's intensity, and the rich gravy's seemingly sweet roasted aromas.
Red Wine Type 2 2008 Château Cissac, Cru Bourgeois 12.5% Vol.	😐 Despite the strong truffle aroma, the tannins come to the fore because there isn't enough fat to counterbalance the rather complex wine.	🙂 The pan-fried fennel and the fatty truffle red wine-butter balance the red wine's tannins, so that the wine can take on the protein in the fish.	😐 The wine isn't mature enough, shows acidity, and seems somewhat rough around the edges. Leather, autumn leaves and undergrowth are the missing aromas for a perfect combination.
Red Wine Type 2 1999 Château Jonqueyres, Bordeaux Supérieur, Double magnum 12.5% Vol.	☹️ The sliced, raw truffle needs a fresher and primary-fruit-dominant partner. Braised and roasted notes to counterbalance the mature wine are missing.	☹️ The advanced maturity collides with the fish protein and brings unpleasant metallic notes forward. The red wine truffle-butter doesn't have enough roasted aromas for this lean, quite mature wine.	🙂 Perfect, because the braised and roasted notes create a delicious bridge to the slightly frail, aged notes, and allow the wine's fruit to come charmingly to the fore.

Note: For over 20 years, the restless truffle expert Ralf Bos has been dealing intensively with truffles from around the world, and sells almost all known varieties on the market through his delicatessen business (www.bosfood.de). For him, winter truffles from the Périgord, as well as the Northern Provence, are among the finest in the world. His personal tip for these experiments: the better the base ingredients, the greater the taste experience!

Buttered Bread with Truffles
Crunchy, Delicious, Earthy and Truffle-Scented

1 loaf of dark bread (rye bread made with 70% sourdough)
200 g good-quality winter truffles (approx. 4 x 50g)
Beurre Baratte au Sel de Mer de Guérande (Butter from Brittany, France)
Fleur de sel
Olive oil (best quality)

Actually, the preparation is self-explanatory: cut four slices of bread (thumb's-width) and spread them generously with butter. The more rustic the bread, the thicker the truffle slices. Using a sharp knife, cut the truffle into thin, approx. two-millimeter-thick slices, and place them amply on each slice of bread. Sprinkle with a fruity, slightly bitter olive oil, and some fleur de sel to taste. By no means serve this right out of the refrigerator. By giving the ingredients of this truffle creation a little time to warm up, a delicious taste experience is guaranteed.

Based on a statement once made by Alain Ducasse—that in addition to the truffle-quality, often the quantity is a problem—Ralf Bos remarks with a wink: "The biggest mistake one can make is to be short of truffles."

Red Wine Type I 🍷
Light and Fresh

What happens?

The truffle is cut into thicker slices because we're using an intensely-flavored artisanal bread. The bread is generously covered with salted butter and truffle slices. This way the truffle meets its catalytic partners "fat" and "salt." Without these ingredients, the truffle wouldn't be able to release its intense flavor in the first place. The grassy, fresh, slightly bitter olive oil also ensures delicate, spicy refreshment and whets the appetite for another bite. The fruity, rather lean Bordeaux with its fruit and refreshing acidity is just the right thing. The slightly rough tannins are smoothed out by the butter's fat content. This light-red wine profits from the earthy truffle aroma, and shows lively fruit and delicious length.

Result:

Here's the chance for simple Bordeaux wines which, with 12.5 percent alcohol, belong to the light-weight red wine types.
They cling in jubilation to the truffled and buttered bread, and develop delicious fruit flavors. Truffles need fat and salt in order

for their flavor to unfold. This flavor-enhancing combination smooths out the sometimes rough-edged tannins, gives the wines more structure, and brings the fruity flavors refreshingly to the fore, thanks to the wine's acidity. The result is a harmonious relationship in which both partners complement each other—which you will not achieve with fuller-bodied, low-acid, red wines.

2006
Château Le Bourdieu,
Cru Bourgeois, Médoc,
France
This bourgeoise find shines with a pleasurable fragrance, stimulating blackberry aromas, some cherry, leather and softly toasted oak, and a pleasantly modern touch. This wine is quite intense, with a refreshingly lively style; noticeable acidity and fruit; dark berry aromas; and an intense tannin backbone. With a pleasant 12.5 percent alcohol content and a medium structure, this is a serious red wine with perfectly integrated alcohol, which leads into a juicy, yet youthfully restrained, expansive length. A freshly fruity, balanced, everyday Bordeaux with good value for the money, it is tasty, uncomplicated and delicious.

Monkfish with Truffle, Fennel and Beurre Rouge
Savory, Earthy, Truffle-Scented and Creamy

4 slices fresh monkfish (120 g)
150 g Beurre Baratte au Sel de Mer de Guérande (Butter from Brittany)
2 shallots
2 bulbs fennel
50 cl red wine (the same wine which is paired with this dish)
Oil for frying
Salt and pepper

2 tbsp finely minced shallots
200 ml red wine (the same wine which is paired with this dish)
200 ml Balsamic vinegar (dark)
200 ml water
½ tsp coriander seeds
½ tsp fennel seeds
½ tsp peppercorns
1 clove
3 Juniper berries
2 Bay leaves
250 g Beurre Baratte au Sel de Mer de Guérande (very cold)
50 ml black truffle juice
50 g black truffles sliced in fine julienne strips

Season the fish well with salt and pepper, and fry in a hot pan with a small amount of oil for approx. three minutes on each side. Then, switch off the stove and let the fish stand. Add a stick of butter, and drape the melted butter over the monkfish slices.

Slice the shallots in fine, julienned strips, and sauté then in butter in a hot pan until they're lightly browned and roasted aromas develop. Add the fennel, and braise together with the shallots until it also turns brown and develops roasted aromas. Then, douse with 50 cl red wine, and finish cooking the fennel until done. Season to taste with a dash of salt.

For the beurre rouge, mince the shallots and lightly sauté them in butter until translucent. Deglaze with red wine, vinegar and water, then add the spices. Reduce to one-quarter of the original amount. Strain, then bind the liquid slowly and carefully with 200 g cold butter. Season to taste with salt and truffle juice. Fold in the truffle strips at the very end, and keep warm.

Red Wine Type 2 🍷🍷
Fruity and Harmonious

What Happens?

In this combination the fennel, with its browned and roasted flavors, takes over a substantial part of the job of buffering the wine's tannins. Together with the roasted shallots; the butter-and-cream-based red wine-sauce; and the truffles, the dish smooths out the somewhat-harsh tannins of the Cru Bourgeois, and brings its fruity aromas charmingly to the fore. The combination of beurre rouge, truffles, and fennel in this case builds a bridge to the more brash tannins of a young, red wine. For the sauce itself, the truffle is cut into thin strips so that it can give as much flavor to the sauce as possible. The shaved truffles are added shortly before serving. In so doing, the truffles reach the necessary temperature, which allows them to develop their bewitching aroma.

Result:

Derived from its symbiosis with the buttery, salty sauce, the truffle takes on a bridge-building effect which, in the first instance, buffers the rough-edged tannins of the young Bordeaux, but then also takes over an additional, vital task. In conjunction with the roasted fennel, this liaison is capable of putting the fish protein, at least sensorially, out of commission. When tannins and proteins are combined, a collision is normally inevitable. Think of fresh goat cheese and red wine-tannins. The delicate alliance between salted butter, truffles and fennel makes the monkfish an exceptionally gifted red wine partner for medium-bodied and not-all-too-mature wines.

2008
Château Cissac,
Cru Bourgeois, Haut-Médoc,
France

Expressive aroma with great depth, delicately spicy, dark berried and multifaceted. This assemblage is composed of two-thirds Cabernet Sauvignon and one-third Merlot and Petit Verdot. It shows typical aromas of black currants; a hint of bell pepper; and wild berries. Still, this wine is somewhat restrained, with lively acidity, subtle cedar notes and juicy tannins which still show some youthful astringency. With its 12.5 percent, the alcohol is very moderate and well-integrated. This is a medium-bodied wine with graceful silkiness and balanced structure, which was aged in both new as well as used barrels. Its complexity and its potential, however, will be revealed only after an appropriate aging period.

Roasted Chicken with Truffles and Celeriac Purée

Roasted, Smooth, Earthy and Truffle-scented

1.5 – 2 kg chicken (whole)
(Mieral-Poultry, Poulet de
Bresse, or others)
120 g black winter truffles, cut
into 2 mm slices
100 ml olive oil
Fleur de sel
1/2 l poultry stock
1 bulb celeriac
1 onion (small)
100 g potatoes
150 g butter
Salt, nutmeg, white pepper
1/2 l poultry stock

Cut into the chicken along its spine so that the skin can be removed, and the truffle slices can be placed on the drumstick, between the skin and the meat. Then, remove the breastbone on the front side. Run your index finger along the edge of the breast, remove the skin, and shove the truffle slices between the skin and the meat. Bring the chicken back into shape. Rub with olive oil and season generously with fleur de sel. Roast for approx. 75 minutes in a 160 degree-Celsius-oven and baste from time to time with its own juice.

For the sauce, another portion of the truffle gets cut into thin, julienned strips. Thin truffle slices would lose their consistency in the hot sauce.

Peel the celeriac, dice and cook with the onion and potato in the poultry stock until soft. Strain off the stock, add butter, and purée with a mixer. Season to taste with salt, pepper and nutmeg. The potato starch allows the purée to bind better.

Red Wine Type 2 🍷🍷
Fruity and Harmonious

What Happens?

The highly concentrated aroma of this combination is incredible. The beguiling fragrance is spicy, toasty, warm, and earthy as it reveals aromas of leaves, undergrowth and roasted chicken. The almost neutral-tasting chicken only begins to unfold its full taste in connection with the crispy skin, which is naturally intensified due to its liaison with the truffle. Parallel to this, the rich, creamy, and earthy celery purée, together with the roasted aromas and the seemingly sweet truffle jus, are seductive. Roasted aromas, truffle notes, fat and salt connect to form a compelling alliance which makes the aging Bordeaux appear more vibrant.

Result:

A classic Bordeaux with typical, leathery notes and a low alcohol-content needs a counteracting food partner to present itself in the appropriate light. These are not your typical Sunday sipping wines. Only when this occasionally rough-edged wine is combined with rich ingredients and earthy truffle aromas will its typical, delicately fruity elegance be revealed. The higher the fat content, and the more flavor-enhancing truffle and roasted aromas there are, the more advanced the wine's maturity can be. Frail, mature wines can even be kissed awake from a deep slumber, acting as if they were made exclusively for truffles. This is an ideal dish to help get this mature Bordeaux back on its feet. Note: one can exceed the limit with some ingredients, but not with truffles. A lack of truffles brings about a bland taste. That would be counter-productively thrifty.

1999
Château Jonqueyres,
Bordeaux Supérieur,
France

This wine contains a gentle fragrance—leathery, dusty aromas that indicate ripeness, leaves, lovage, undergrowth, forest-floor and a hint of licorice. The once-vibrant primary fruit-flavors have evolved significantly in the direction of maturity. On the palate there are faint oak notes as well as soft aromas of ripe and dark berries which are supported by a refreshing acidity. The wine glides smoothly over the palate, isn't particularly complex, but pleasantly elegant, harmonious and has a medium-long finish. The alcohol of 12.5 percent is moderate and very well integrated.

Hot Temptation

Meets Sweet Taste

Four different curry sauces with varying degrees of spice will be served with the same base dish. The varying spice levels–from mild to very hot–are paired with four different sweet Riesling types from Kabinett, Spätlese and Auslese to a Beerenauslese.

While sweet is a flavor, sensations such as spicy, hot, cool, astringent or tingling aren't directly perceived by the taste receptors, but are passed via stimulation to the cranial trigeminal nerve.

> The sharpness of hot spice
> is not a taste, but an irritation.

Chili, for instance, generates a hot impression. You blow air over your tongue as if the food is hot in temperature, but the sensation being experienced is actually sharp, a sensation created by pain. A popular remedy to this is yogurt; indeed, it cools and soothes.

So according to which criteria should you search for the right wine-match for spice? Eiswein, for example, can't necessarily score points with spicy food. Its high sugar-concentration is an advantage, but depending on the degree of spice, it could be a difficult match with its extremely high acidity. But the sweet direction is principally the right one. Therefore, it is a good idea to focus on the combination of sweet, fruity Riesling and different residual sugar levels in order to demonstrate that with increasing sweetness, a corresponding level of spicy heat can be buffered.

Experiment:

Four different curry sauces with varying degrees of spice will be made with the same main ingredients: tiger prawns and vegetables. The four different degrees of spicy heat get matched with four Rieslings of different sweetness levels. The severity of spicy heat increases with every dish from mildly spicy, medium-spicy, spicy-hot to very spicy-hot. For each of the different types of sweet Riesling, Kabinett, Spätlese, Auslese and Beerenauslese, there are four different demand profiles. The respective heat level is paired with each of the different wine types of ascending sweetness levels. Try each dish with each wine. Find out which Riesling, at which sweetness level, offers the best alliance to which degree of spicy heat.

How does spicy heat react to sweetness? Curry (mild to hot) and Riesling (fruity-sweet to noble-sweet)	
Curry Sauce, Mild Jaipur curry	**Sweet Wine Type 1** Riesling Kabinett, light and fresh (55 g residual sugar/l)
Curry Sauce, Piquant Thai curry, green	**Sweet Wine Type 2** Riesling Spätlese, fruity and harmonious (91 g residual sugar/l)
Curry Sauce, Hot Thai curry, red	**Sweet Wine Type 3** Riesling Auslese, complex and elegant (108 g residual sugar/l)
Curry Sauce, Very Hot Goa curry	**Sweet Wine Type 4** Riesling Beerenauslese, powerful and opulent (219 g residual sugar/l)

(Experiment)

Note:

When using hot spices (e.g., curry or chili), the type of preparation or the choice of meat is less important than the particular spicy heat-level. In general, wines with a fine fruit-acid balance; low alcohol-content; and corresponding sweetness are perfectly suitable for spicy dishes. The more severe the spicy heat, the more intense the sweetness must be. Wines with sweetness and fruit have an affinity for spicy heat–but only to a certain degree. This delicate construct can eventually be thrown out of balance as soon as the wine's sweetness becomes too overpowering and cloying.

Wine pairing:

The appropriate wine accompaniment, in this case, is made from a single grape variety, from one appellation and by the same producer. According to the Prädikat, a German classification system describing wine types, here are the sugar levels of Riesling in ascending order: Kabinett 55 g/l, Spätlese 91g/l, Auslese 108 g/l and Beerenauslese 219 g/l. Sweet wine types with all of these different levels are most likely found at a winery in the Mosel, Ruwer, the Saar, Nahe or the Rheingau. "Each sweet wine types has, in regards to taste, a perceptibly different degree of sweetness."

Matter of taste:

You should take some time for this complex experiment. The ingredients for all four curry sauces should be ready so that you can cook each sauce *à la minute*. But before you begin to prepare the sauces, it is advisable to taste the wines first, because in connection with the food–depending on the degree of spicy heat–their taste will undergo extreme changes. The distinction is relatively clear. As opposed to sweetness, which can be tasted, spicy heat can only be experienced as a painful stimulus. How does the wine's sweetness handle this irritation? What happens to its vibrant fruit flavors?

	Curry - Mild Jaipur curry	Curry - Piquant Thai, green	Curry - Hot Thai, red	Curry - Very Hot Goa
Sweet Wine Type 1 2009 Wehlener Sonnenuhr Riesling Kabinett Geheimrat J. Wegeler, Mosel, Germany 55 g/l RS | 7.8 TA | 9% Vol.	🙂 This Kabinett wine seems much drier and very quaffable. Residual sugar and spice even each other out.	😐 Lively spiciness from the ethereal notes of the green curry. Unfortunately not enough sweetness for the piquant spice; the wine turns short and dry.	🙁 The delicate Kabinett has no chance against the red Thai curry. It loses its fruit, and seems short and dry.	🙁 The wine's delicately fruity notes are displaced by the hot spice with astringent and metallic notes.
Sweet Wine Type 2 2009 Wehlener Sonnenuhr Riesling Spätlese Geheimrat J. Wegeler, Mosel, Germany 91 g/l RS | 7.4 TA | 8% Vol.	😐 The gentle, hot spice lets the Spätlese show off its aromas, pushing them to the fore. It seems a bit too sweet, though.	🙂 More pizzaz! The refreshing, piquant spice of the green curry lends the Spätlese a veritably fruity appeal.	🙁 Chili gives piquant, hot spice, which demands too much of the harmonious Spätlese and steals its fruit flavors, due to its lacks of sweetness.	🙁 This curry mixture is much too spicy-hot for the fruity Spätlese. Fruit is lost, acidity is pushed to the fore, and seems metallic.
Sweet Wine Type 3 2009 Wehlener Sonnenuhr Riesling Auslese Geheimrat J. Wegeler, Mosel, Germany 108 g/l RS | 8.4 TA | 8% Vol.	🙁 The mild Jaipur curry is too gentle for the explosively fruity Auslese. Spice is lacking to balance out the intensive sweetness. The sweetness seems like an insurmountable barrier.	😐 Refreshingly piquant hot spice, the ethereal notes from the green curry provide a link to the sweet Auslese. But the curry should have a touch more heat.	🙂 The complex Auslese seems to be tailor-made for the curry's spice level. It lets the lively fruit aromas and fine, polished elegance shine through.	🙁 Goa packs quite a punch with its spicy heat, steals the fruit aromas and, most of all, the elegance from this complex Auslese.
Sweet Wine Type 4 2009 Wehlener Sonnenuhr Riesling Beerenauslese Geheimrat J. Wegeler, Mosel, Germany 219 g/l RS | 9.4 TA | 8% Vol.	🙁 You get the feeling that this opulent Beerenauslese simply ignores the curry. It's much too sweet.	😐 The curry's refreshing spice gets a brief moment of attention, but all in all it doesn't have enough power for the Beerenauslese's concentration of fruit and sweetness.	🙁 Even though the red Thai curry paste packs quite a punch, the Beerenauslese simply remains sweet, and shows too little of its elegance and fruit.	🙂 Finally! The 219 grams of sugar are integrated. The sweetness masks the hot spice perfectly. Fruit, liveliness and elegance are the delicious reward.

Note: Spice expert Ingo Holland didn't just supply the curry spices for this experiment, he very kindly cooked the dishes himself. Moreover, he is one of the few chefs who knows what he's talking about when cooking a dish to match a specific wine. His extensive range of spices and seminars can be found on: **www.ingo-holland.de**.

The Base Dish

Brown the eggplant diamonds on all sides in hot olive oil in a large pan. Tip the eggplant into a sieve, and squeeze out the oil. Heat the pan again, add the drained oil, and briefly sauté the carrots first, followed by the leeks, and then the snow peas, so that they don't take on color and become limp. Add the eggplant to the vegetables, then the bamboo shoots and soybean sprouts. Toss together quickly, and season with salt.

Salt the tiger prawns, and sprinkle with Espelette chili. Heat the olive oil in a pan, brown the prawns on one side then flip over, adding butter. Baste prawns several times with the foaming butter. Cooking time for each side is approximately two minutes. Distribute the vegetables onto deep plates, place one prawn on each plate. These should only be tasting-size portions, since you will have to taste and eat each portion four times with different sauces!

Afterward, prepare the corresponding sauce (see sauce recipes), then emulsify and froth them up with an immersion blender. Drizzle each dish generously with the sauce, and garnish with deep-fried chili filaments. Serve hot.

Sautéed Tiger Prawns on Thai Vegetables

2 small eggplants (cut into 2-3 cm long diamond-shaped pieces)
1 leek (only the green part, sliced in 1 cm rings)
2 carrots, medium (2 mm thick slices)
2 handfuls fresh soybean sprouts
100 g bamboo shoots (in strips)
4 cloves garlic (finely minced)
100 g snow peas (cut diagonally in 2-3 cm lengths)
100 ml olive oil
Rock salt

16 peeled and deveined tiger prawns (if possible wild catch, head removed, 8/12 calibration)
Rock salt
2 tsp Espelette chili (Piment d'Espelette)
2 tbsp olive oil
2 pieces of butter (walnut sized)
Several chili filaments
200 ml deep-frying fat

Jaipur Curry, mild
Refreshingly Piquant, Gentle Heat

1 tbsp peanut oil
1 heaping tbsp shallots or onions (minced)
1 heaping tsp tomato paste
1 tsp Jaipur curry
200 ml coconut milk
200 ml heavy cream
Cane sugar, to taste
Lemon juice
Asian fish sauce (preferably Squid Brand)
Rock salt as desired

Jaipur Curry

This spice contains fenugreek, coriander, turmeric, cumin, chili, lemon grass, ginger, fennel, brown mustard, black pepper, cardamom, garlic, mace, galangal and cinnamon flower, among other spices.

Heat peanut oil in a deep pan, add shallots, sauté until translucent, add tomato paste and stir continuously so that it doesn't turn color. Add Jaipur curry-powder and sauté slowly with the onions at low heat. Careful: never add curry powder directly to hot oil, for it will burn and develop a bitter taste.

The curry spice only truly develops and unfolds its full flavor during the gentle cooking process. Add the coconut milk (make sure to shake it up first) as well as the heavy cream to the pan, and boil down. The desired reduction consistency is when the sauce has reached an approximate quarter-liter final volume. Remove from the stove and season to taste with sugar; fish sauce (not too sparingly); lemon juice; and salt. Emulsify with an immersion blender.

Heat through, and serve with the prawns and vegetables. Unlike Thai curry sauce, this curry sauce is somewhat thicker, due to the tomato paste.

Sweet Wine Type I 🍷
Light and Fresh

What Happens?

The curry sauce has a delicate sweetness from the sautéed onions and the lightly roasted tomato paste in olive oil. The sauce's umami stems from the fermented anchovies found in the fish sauce and the concentrated tomato paste. The coconut cream lends a gentle texture and delicate sweetness. The fish sauce provides saltiness, and the lemon juice a balancing acidity. The combination of salt and acid is ideal as a natural flavor-enhancer. The gentle Jaipur curry can unfold beautifully among these balancing components. Ginger and garlic from the curry mixture also results in a delicious accord in this combination, and receives refreshing support from coriander, fennel and lemon grass. The prawns and the vegetables buffer the chili's gentle, spicy heat.

Result:

The result is a harmonious, very gentle, spicy heat, which has a stimulating effect and supports the flavor of the shrimp and the vegetables.

The residual sugar content of 55 grams per liter not only buffers the wine's acidity, but also buffers the gentle spice perfectly. The Kabinett seems drier and extremely quaffable. The relatively high residual sugar-content (compared to dry wines) masks the spicy heat or, rather, simply levels it. At the same time, the serving temperature of 8 degrees Celsius has a cooling effect on the palate.

2009 Wehlener Sonnenuhr Riesling Kabinett, Geheimrat J. Wegeler, Mosel, Germany (55 g/l RS | 7.8 TA | 9% Vol.)

This wine has a delicate, stimulating aroma of apple, peach, and a touch of honeydew melon. It is lightly herbal and somewhatdusty, but with a very crisp, lively acidity, which lets the fruit sweetness dance on the tongue. This Kabinett is in the beginning stage of its maturity. The aromas are still showing sweet-sour characteristics, and will develop a delicious harmony and fine fruity juiciness with appropriate cellaring. This is a gently woven, light and very refreshing Riesling which still has many years ahead of it, and which really doesn't seem capable of standing up to a spicy meal.

Thai Green Curry, Piquant
Refreshing, Pleasantly Pungent Spice

1 tbsp peanut oil
40 g Thai green curry paste
400 ml coconut milk
1 tsp cane sugar
Lime juice from ½ lime
Asian fish sauce (preferably Squid Brand)
Rock salt as desired

Thai Green Curry Paste

This paste contains green chili, galangal, lemon grass, garlic, shallots, coriander, coriander roots, lime rind, lime zest, lime leaves, nutmeg and cumin, among other spices.

Heat peanut oil in a deep pan, add curry paste, and gently sauté, stirring continuously with a wooden spoon so that it doesn't turn color. Add approx. one-half cup of the coconut milk (make sure to shake it up first) to the pan and boil down, then fill up the pan with the remaining coconut milk and reduce anew.

After a short reduction time, the sauce should have an approximate one-quarter liter final volume. Remove from the stove and season to taste with sugar, lime, fish sauce (not too sparingly), and if necessary, salt. Emulsify with an immersion blender. Heat through and serve with the prawns and vegetables. Thai curry sauces are never very thick, but rather are served with a runny consistency.

Sweet Wine Type 2 🍷🍷
Fruity and Harmonious

What Happens?

Also here, the curry gets gently roasted because only through heat and the roasting process can the aromas truly unfold. It shouldn't get too hot because otherwise the curry will burn. The sweet-tasting onion flavor in the shallots is already contained in the green Thai curry paste. There are also fresh, ethereal citrus aromas such as lemon grass, coriander, lime peel, lime zest and lime leaves, as well as spicy, warm notes such as cumin and gentle, spicy heat from garlic and green chili. The curry sauce lives from its citrusy, ethereal, very pleasant pungency, which is enhanced by the freshly squeezed lime juice, the fish sauce (umami) and the rock salt. Also here, the prawns and the vegetables buffer the green chili's gentle, spicy heat. You can cut down the hot spice as desired with the velvety smooth coconut milk; it combines all of these components very sensitively with a fat content of a mere 18 percent, which is far less than that of the cream (30 percent) or crème fraîche (approx. 40 percent).

Result:

The green curry sauce provides with its ethereal, citrusy fresh aromas a perfect link to the lively Spätlese, which literally dances across your tongue. Due to its acidity, it hardly seems sweet, although it has a considerable residual sugar content of 91 g/l. The green curry's lemony aromas play to this delicate, elegant sweet wine type considerably better than a red curry. The stimulating aromatics gently support the dish with piquant spice, whereas the sweetness masks the spice's heat and, thus, enables the lively animating fruit aromas to unfold.

2009 Wehlener Sonnenuhr Riesling Spätlese, Geheimrat J. Wegeler, Mosel, Germany
(91 g/l RS | 7.4 TA | 8% Vol.)

This wine type is characterized by delicate, stimulating aromas of, apple, peach and a touch of honeydew melon. It is lightly herbal, somewhat smoky and dusty. Stimulating, cutting acidity, which deliciously supports the fruit aromas along with the enticing sweetness, lets it vibrate on the tongue. This Spätlese presents itself from its multifaceted side with prancing lightness. It will profit from further bottle-age with the individual components converging harmoniously, developing a fine fruitiness, juiciness and drinkability. A typical Mosel-Spätlese with medium intensity, gently woven, delicious and delicate. A wonderfully refreshing wine of which one could, without hesitation, drink more than one glass because fruit, acidity and sweetness are combined in an extremely lively and delicious way.

Thai Red Curry, Spicy
Spicy, Hot, Sharp Spice, and Stimulating Warmth

1 tbsp peanut oil
50 g Thai red curry paste
400 ml coconut milk
1 tsp cane sugar
Lime juice from ½ lime
Asian fish sauce (preferably
Squid Brand)
Rock salt as desired

Thai Red Curry Paste

This paste contains red dried Thai chili, galangal, lemon grass, garlic, shallots, coriander, coriander roots, lime rind, lime zest, lime leaves, nutmeg and cumin, among other spices

Heat peanut oil in a deep pan, add curry paste, and gently sauté, stirring continuously with a wooden spoon so that it doesn't turn color. Add approx. one-half cup of the coconut milk (make sure to shake it up first) to the pan and boil down, then fill up the pan with the remaining coconut milk, and reduce anew.

After a short reduction time the sauce should have an approximate one-quarter liter final volume. Remove from the stove and season to taste with sugar, lime, fish sauce (not too sparingly) and, if necessary, salt. Emulsify with an immersion blender.

Heat through and serve with the prawns and vegetables. Thai curry sauces are never very thick, but rather are served with a runny consistency.

Red Thai curry sauce should be somewhat spicier than the green sauce. To increase the spicy heat of the sauce, simply increase the amount of paste in the recipe. Anise basil, coriander and curry leaves can be added as desired.

Sweet Wine Type 3 🍷🍷🍷
Elegant and Complex

What happens?

Although its basis is red Thai curry with chili, the lemon grass, cilantro, lime zest, lime leaves and grated lime peel provide an ethereal, lemony aroma. Spicy, warm notes of cumin and nutmeg round out the flavor, and release an animatingly spicy kick at the end that, despite its noticeable heat, stimulates the appetite and reverberates pleasantly. Also, this curry sauce benefits from the lemony-ethereal aromas which are soporifically supported by the lime juice, fish sauce (umami) and rock salt. You can minimize the spicy heat with the mildly sweet coconut milk; it combines all of these components very sensitively with its fat component. If you need more spicy heat, just add a little more curry paste to the sauce.

Result:

The curry's hot sensation has a pleasant effect on the aftertaste, briefly coats the palate, and takes over with an appetizing effect. Our Auslese is almost a bit too delicate, and could easily have a few more grams of sugar, but the tiger prawns' protein and the vegetables' starch create a buffer zone for the acidity. This wine contains juicy, ripe apricot notes; dense creaminess; and vibrant fruit on the finish, which, when combined with the spices and the spicy heat, provide a sensational taste experience! The sauce's spicy heat balances the sweetness. It's a combination in which the appeal doesn't stem from a harmonious liaison, but from polarity or contrast. The sweetness offsets the spicy heat, and both cancel each other out, yielding a balanced whole.

2009 Wehlener Sonnenuhr Riesling Auslese, Geheimrat J. Wegeler, Mosel
(108 g/l RS | 8.4 TA | 8% Vol.)

This wine has quite an intense fragrance with apricot and honey aromas which are very concentrated, dense and incredibly complex. The sweetness is perfectly balanced by lively acidity, lending the multifaceted Auslese a stimulating, quaffable and juicy intensity. The long finish presents initial flavors of ripe apricots, orange zest and Kumquat jam, which linger for an immensely long time on the palate. A youthful, powerful, elegant Auslese with vibrant aromas and matching brilliance, this wine type possesses the potential for long-term cellaring and leaves you wanting another glass.

Curry Goa, Very Spicy
Very Hot Spice

1 tbsp peanut oil
1 heaping tbsp shallots or
onions (minced)
100 g canned tomatoes
1 heaping tsp curry Goa
300 ml coconut milk
100 ml heavy cream
Cane sugar, to taste
Lemon juice
Asian fish sauce (preferably
Squid Brand)
Rock salt as desired

Goa Curry

This curry spice contains black pepper, fenugreek, chili, turmeric, coriander, cumin, rose paprika, sweet paprika, star anise, fennel, cardamom, mustard, ginger, galangal, black cumin, mace, long pepper, lemon grass, cloves and cinnamon flower.

Heat peanut oil in a deep pan, add minced shallots, sauté until translucent, add canned tomatoes, stirring continuously so that it doesn't turn color. Add Goa curry powder, and reduce the liquid until it separates from the fat. Careful: never add curry powder directly to hot oil, for it will burn and develop a bitter taste.

The curry spice only truly develops and unfolds its full flavor during the gentle cooking process. Add the coconut milk (make sure to shake it up first), as well as the heavy cream to the pan, and boil down. The desired reduction consistency occurs when the sauce has reached an approximate one-quarter liter final volume. Remove from the stove, and season to taste with sugar, lime, fish sauce (not too sparingly) and, if necessary, a little salt. Emulsify with an immersion blender. Heat through and serve with the prawns and vegetables.

Sweet Wine Type 4 🍷🍷🍷🍷
Powerful and Opulent

What Happens?

The shallots serve as the base, getting lightly sautéed and deglazed with the sweet-tasting juicy tomatoes (umami). Now the spicy Goa curry comes into play: everything is reduced until the liquid separates from the fat. Only then does the coconut milk's soothing influence and the flavor-enhancing effect of lime juice, salt and fish sauce join in. The components are mutually reinforcing, and clear the way for the spicy-hot ingredients (black pepper, chili, rose paprika and mustard). There are also refreshing, ethereal components such as ginger, lemon grass, cloves and cinnamon flowers, which lend the curry, along with its intense heat, a spicy aroma. The interaction between fruit, salt, beguiling sweetness and bracing acidity brings freshness and puts the spicy heat in the right light, thereby giving the combination the necessary pep.

Result:

This powerful, sweet wine type copes very well with the spicy heat. Interestingly, the wine's sweetness steps back completely as it evens out the spicy heat, and in its place the juicy fruit flavors are brought to the fore. The more severe the spicy heat in a sauce or dish, the more intense the wine's sweetness must be. Wines with sweetness and fruit get along with spicy heat!

2009 Wehlener Sonnenuhr Riesling Beerenauslese 103°, Geheimrat J. Wegeler, Mosel, Germany
(219 g/l RS | 9.4 TA | 8% Vol.)

Intense notes of dried apricot, orange marmalade and honey can be found in this wine. Behind the brilliant aroma concentration, this Beerenauslese shines with citrus, pineapple, mango and very lively acidity. It just has to, for the high residual sugar-content would simply be cloying-

ly sweet if it weren't balanced by an appropriate acidity. Imagine if you had to taste 219 grams of sugar dissolved in one liter of water. This is the equivalent to a sugar content of more than 20 percent, and would just taste sickly sweet if there wasn't any balancing acidity involved. The lively balance between fruit, sweetness and acidity is what makes it so special, and lends this extremely rich, sweet wine type its unique charm. Despite this Beerenauslese's high level of sweetness, it seems almost youthful and seductively profound, while at the same time lively and playful.

Unwritten

Rules

Friend and Foe

Practical Rules of Thumb for Promising Partnerships

Wine and food can get caught in a veritable relationship trap. Who can live with whom? Which partners have the right chemistry, and which ones don't? What follows is some vinophile relationship counseling for mortal enemies and faithful partners.

Let's divide food into two groups. The first group is comprised of food which absolutely does not pair well with wine, unless it is combined with buffering ingredients to create an overall harmonious food composition. One should pay extra attention when using these incompatible "loners" in combination with wine. The second group is comprised of companionable foods which are happy to be partnered with the right wine, and also express this in terms of taste. These are classical and, for the most part, culturally evolved, combinations. It is worth knowing these, for with these combinations one is usually on the right track.

So in this chapter we will consider the question, friend or foe? Besides examining foods which call for a cold beer rather than wine, we will concentrate on the truly delicate food and wine combinations. It will be explained in detail, why a combination works and why it does not. While pickled herring upstages every wine and prefers a cold beer as a partner, juicy white asparagus cuddles up deliciously with a crisp Silvaner. White wine, rather than red wine, is a much friendlier match with cheese—this is not known to many. Meanwhile, chocolate, depending on its type, is fond of white and also red wine. And do you actually know why Pinot Noir goes so well with a fatty, roast goose?

What does one need to know in order to match food and wine successfully?

Before you read on, you must be warned. You will need patience as well as a good portion of curiosity and, most of all, lots of time to taste, in order to gain the necessary combination competence. Moreover, this pastime can develop into a true passion—not to mention an unavoidable calorie consumption.

Foes

As a basic principle: there is food which practically never goes well with wine, at least in its raw or pure state. In combination with wine, their incompatible components converge, which has a disastrous effect on flavor. These foods are–if at all–only compatible with wine when combined with buffering elements which offset and counterbalance the extreme substances.

Friends

In the case of friendly relationships between wine and food, it is generally a matter of traditional, usually regional, matches which have evolved historically and culturally over centuries. With respect to food and beverage culture, France is a few steps ahead of other countries. Just think of fruits de mer with a lively Muscadet, or beef bourguignon with an elegant Pinot Noir. But actually, there are exciting examples all over the world. These combinations will seldom fail, because they have been tested over the course of generations.

Note: These lists should merely serve as a guideline, and are by no means exhaustive. For example, sauerkraut (actually a wine-pairing foe) in combination with other food can go perfectly well with wine (see Choucroute & Alsatian Riesling). Despite all the proven theories, this still holds true: you must taste and learn what will proverbially captivate your senses, versus what will make you lose your appetite. Taste is influenced by the interaction of food-chemical parameters, as well as by the rules and cultural experiences which we, and our ancestors, have learned and gathered.

Foes	Friends
Artichokes	Seafood & Muscadet
Spinach	White Asparagus & Silvaner
Tomatoes	Maultaschen & Trollinger
Fruit	Goat Cheese & Sancerre
Radishes, red or white	Coq au Vin & Beaujolais
Wasabi	Munster Cheese & Gewürztraminer
Mustard	Cheese Fondue & Fendant
Pickled Herring	Stilton Cheese & Port
Sauerkraut	Choucroute & Alsatian Riesling
Yogurt	Entrecôte & Bordeaux
Ice Cream	Beef Bourguignon & Pinot Noir
Coffee	Foie Gras & Noble Sweet Wine

Foes

Artichokes (cooked)

The high level of bitter compounds makes life difficult for an accompanying wine. Every wine must capitulate to cooked artichoke. The wine develops harsh, utterly metallic notes. It also loses all fruit aromas, tastes simple, thin and acidic. Residual sugar sticks out mercilessly and the tannins in red wine intensify, becoming bitter and astringent.

The artichoke's bitter compounds, cynarin, prevent the perception of fruit aromas on the back of the palate because they coat the relevant olfactory receptors. This way, they overpower the delicate fruit aromas. To reduce the bitterness, artichokes are usually cooked in salt water with lemon juice. How does this work? Lemon juice makes the water sour and helps, as the water boils, to break down the bitter cynarin.

The compatibility between artichokes and wine therefore depends highly on the method of cooking–and also on the sauce with which the artichokes are served.

Spinach (raw)

Spinach has a relatively high acidity, and also contains oxalic crystals. These tiny crystals coat the tongue, teeth and the entire palate. They are responsible for the uncomfortably rough impression–similar to the tannins of a young red wine–which coats the palate. When pure spinach (particularly when raw) is served with wine, the acidity and oxalic crystals collide unrelentingly with the wine's tannins, thereby causing a tannin explosion. With juicy, fresh wines, any delicate fruit aromas are virtually destroyed, whereas barrique-aged wines, due to their present tannins, generally interact well with raw spinach.

When spinach is cooked, these different wine types have to struggle less and are able to show decidedly more fruit. During the cooking process, the oxalic crystals are broken down and remain in the cooking water. In combination with cooked spinach, the wine's fruit aromas can once again come to the fore.

Red wine with young, expressive tannins copes particularly well with the effect of the oxalic crystals. It is simply the acidity in spinach which can pose problems for this type of wine. Its finish becomes dull, clumsy and shows woody notes.

Tomatoes (raw)

The acidity and the green, vegetal, bitter impression of raw tomatoes immediately sends wine into a tailspin. The culprit, besides the acidity, is the alkaloid called solanin (also called tomatin). The tomato's bitterness emphasizes the acidic components in wine, and forms an impenetrable barrier. Light wines lose all their fruit, fall apart and just taste sour. But heavier wines react to the bitterness of this red fruit with an acidic taste. Tannins become rough and seem astringent, while the alcohol unpleasantly comes to the fore with a sweet impression.

Tomatoes in dried form, or as a tomato coulis, are highly concentrated and act as a natural flavor enhancer, contributing their inherent umami as an ingredient to pleasantly season a dish. In the case of ketchup or barbecue sauces (which all contain concentrated tomato paste) the meaning of this statement changes. These industrially manufactured products contain not only natural (umami) as well as artificial (glutamate) flavor enhancers, but also a great deal of sugar. For this reason, pairing barbecue sauce with wine can prove to be challenging, so a fresh, draft beer oftentimes pairs better with the sauce's sweetness. You can, however, use this knowledge to add some pizzazz to a simple, soft red wine by pairing it with ketchup or tomatoes.

Fruit (raw and acidic)

Most fruit varieties contain not only fruit sugar (fructose), but also a significant amount of acid. These components can clash, for they are also present in a wine. So in this case, birds of a feather won't flock together. Depending on the fruit variety, its ripeness, sugar content and acidity, raw fruit and wine can be polarizing due to the competition which occurs on the palate. So when fruit is raw and acidic, it dominates every wine, while cooked fruit is much easier to pair with wine. Why is this so? When exposed to heat, the aggressive acids either metabolize or evaporate.

Dijon Mustard

Due to its pungent character, mustard affects wine much like wasabi and horseradish. The combination of sweetness (added sugar), acidity and spice takes a dominant role in this case. For this reason, mustard is, just like wasabi and horseradish, only compatible with wine when it is in a milder form (e.g., as a seasoning for sauces and marinades, etc). The mustard's sugar content elicits an unpleasant sweetness in wine. Again, in this combination, a chilled lager is the better match. Beer cuts through much of mustard's pungency, and never loses its original flavor.

Radishes, red and white (raw)

All species of horseradish; white and red radish; turnips; their sprouts as well as wasabi are very problematic wine partners due to their acidity, bitter compounds, pungency and essential oils. A radish's intrinsic pungency comes from the ingredient allyl isothiocyanate (AITC). Wasabi stands alone in this group and is, in its pure form, completely incompatible with wine due to its extreme pungency. It destroys any and all of a wine's fruit and aromatics, and coats the palate with an unpleasant bitterness. AITC is considerably more aggressive than the delicate fruit aromas, and it quickly coats the relevant olfactory receptors. The subtle fruit aromas don't have a chance of being noticed. Alcohol reacts neutrally and remains in the background. This is the result of the competitive situation in which the pungency prevents the alcohol from coming to the fore.

Note: a fresh draft beer is a superb match with these pungent foods. Maltose, a sugar present in beer, helps to tone down the pungency considerably—and in spite of this, the beer doesn't lose its flavor. This is certainly a reason why a typical Bavarian snack of white or red radishes, or horseradish is traditionally paired with a fresh, draft beer. In Asia, where the cuisine is incredibly spicy (and for most Europeans, intolerable), beer as well as sweet Riesling is often served. A kind of all-around solution for wine lovers is that wine with lots of fruit and sweetness (fructose) goes well with hot spices—but only to a certain degree. The theory thereby holds that the hotter the spice, the more sweetness is needed in the wine. But

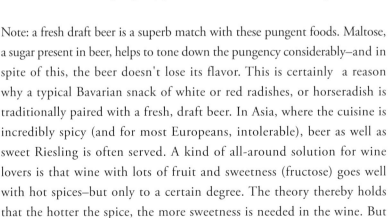

a word of caution: this delicate construct can eventually be thrown out of balance as soon as the wine's sweetness becomes too overpowering and cloying. In the end, this still holds true: tasting always tops theorizing. The proof is on your palate.

Anchovies

Anchovies are somewhat smaller than sardines, but also belong to the herring family. They shouldn't be confused with the milder-tasting sprats. They are widely used as a seasoning ingredient in southern and central European cuisine. Anchovies are cut into fillets, preserved with salt and then left to mature, in some cases for many years, until they achieve a soft consistency. During this maturation period the fish ferments, producing the natural flavor enhancer umami. Due to the intense aromas, these anchovies are only compatible with wine when combined with other buffering ingredients. They're mostly used—as a paste or in small fillets—as a seasoning ingredient with an intense fish taste.

Sauerkraut

The sour taste of raw, fermented white cabbage and the lactic acid it contains are not compatible with wine. Light, crisp wines develop an aggressive acidity and lose their fruit aromas. Fuller-bodied, barrique-aged white wines appear alcoholic, broad and sweetish, while red wine completely falls apart and becomes unpleasantly soft and one-dimensional. It's only when hearty pork roast, Nürnberger bratwurst, bacon, sausages, boiled potatoes or creamy mashed potatoes join the table, that sauerkraut's acidic taste gets buffered. Practical tip: you can reverse this argument and use the sauerkraut's qualities to help a full-bodied wine with low acidity become more lively.

Pickled Herring

A good pickled herring is particularly tender and fatty. Pickled herring is traditionally stored in barrels and preserved in a salty brine. It can be identified by its pale, marzipan-colored flesh. Fresh pickled herring stands out by its aromas, reminiscent of the sea and algae with hints of butter as well as a viscous, mildly salty, iodine-like, mouth-filling taste. These characteristics, together with the fat content, densely coat the mouth with pickled herrings' unique flavor. Whoever has ever tried to pair pickled herring and wine will have, at some point, given up in frustration and turned to a cool beer. A wine's fruit aromas categorically fall apart and are transformed into unpleasant, sweetish and also bitter characteristics. While every wine fails the compatibility test, a beer's lightly sweet and bitter notes are the perfect, refreshing accompaniment to the intense pickled herring taste and helps to prepare one's palate for the next bite. Beer absorbs the fat content much better than wine. This also applies to spirits, by the way. Just think of a good Aquavit.

Yogurt

Wine is usually incapable of breaking through the creamy taste of yogurt. The mouth becomes completely plastered with the cool, sour and fatty sensation. There is, unfortunately, no room for a good sip of wine. In the full sense of the word: Yogurt suppresses the wine's aromas and intensifies all its unpleasant characteristics. A similar reaction is caused by nonfat quark (a typical German milk product) which influences wine very much like yogurt. This situation changes completely as soon as the quark has a higher fat and salt content. Consider, for example, rich cream cheese made of cow's or goat's milk, which is an excellent match for fruity, delicate sweet wines. Herbed quark or cottage cheese and jacket potatoes are best accompanied by a fresh draft beer—the savory hops flavors and the sweet maltiness are perfect complements.

Ice Cream

This delicacy gives every wine the cold shoulder. The reasons for this aren't just the high sugar and fat content, but, above all, the temperature. The cold restricts all sense of smell and taste. Hence, the long-cultivated custom of serving sorbet between the appetizer and the main course is, in fact, disastrous for the accompanying wine. Sorbet is indeed a tongue-torturer, and has a negative impact on the subsequent wine and its aromas. Further aggravation is caused by a wine's tannins, which become perceptibly more intense at cold temperatures. In combination with red wine, an ice cream bomb turns into a tannin bomb!

Coffee

True: coffee's aftertaste clings to the palate for a long time and ultimately overpowers all other aromas!

False: coffee ruins one's sensory capacity for wine for at least 30 minutes. On the contrary—at first, coffee serves as a catalyst, intensifying one's sensory perception by emphasizing fruit aromas and acidity impression.

Nevertheless, a coffee aftertaste can't be suppressed and, with respect to wine, has the final say and sticks around to the bitter end. A young, fruity red wine with a medium tannin level shows its attributes in high definition when consumed after a cup of coffee. Not only that, in this case, coffee and wine complement each other perfectly. Fresh, dark-berry fruit; a lively acidity; as well as chocolaty, toasty aromas unfold and shine simultaneously. This experiment was undertaken with espresso coffee. A drip coffee, due to the extended contact with coffee grounds, will certainly have an elevated bitterness, especially when it has been kept warm over a longer period.

Friends

Seafood and Muscadet

Muscadet is a simple and uncomplicated wine, whose appeal stems from a crisp acidity, light style and delicate yeastiness. It tastes fresh and fruity with aromas of apple and citrus. This clear, lively taste is a perfect partner with seafood and shellfish, which are usually served raw or cooked briefly in salt-water.

Asparagus and Silvaner

Asparagus is acid-averse, reacting with unpleasant, bitter, metallic notes. And since it is seldom eaten on its own, classic accompaniments such as hollandaise sauce, melted butter and potatoes also play a role. One therefore needs a wine which not only has delicate fruit, but also adequate body and viscosity in order to cope with the vegetal aromas, as well as with fat and starch. These attributes are present in Silvaner, making it a perfect partner whose quality is often enhanced in combination with asparagus.

Maultaschen and Trollinger

Maultaschen (literally translated to mean "mouth pockets") are a Swabian culinary specialty made of pasta dough filled with a ground meat, spinach, onions and *brewis* (soaked breadrolls). They are either cooked in boiling water and served on their own, or enjoyed swimming in meat broth as a soup. Furthermore, cooked maultaschen are often served with brown butter and caramelized onions. The best match for this home-style, rather rich dish is a fruity, uncomplicated Trollinger whose low tannins and pleasant acidity are stimulating, and make you crave the next bite.

Goat Cheese and Sancerre

The white wine of Sancerre (Sauvignon Blanc) and the goat cheese Crottin de Chavignol carry the geographic origin designation of Appellation d'Origine Contrôlée (AOC) and are only allowed to be produced in the region of Sancerre. The cheese can taste either mild, tart, lightly nutty or almost creamy-chalky, depending on the season and its maturity. A fruit-driven Sauvignon Blanc with grassy aromas and a stimulating acidity pairs best with these intense aromas. Both the wine and the cheese retain their original characteristics and complement each other perfectly.

Coq au Vin and Beaujolais

Coq au Vin (French for "Rooster in Wine") is considered one of France's national dishes. There are certainly a multitude of recipe variations, but the classic version has its roots in Burgundy. Chicken parts which were marinated in red wine are browned with bacon and onions. Then they are braised gently in a cast iron pot with herbs, spices and a light, fruity red wine. This can be a fresh Burgundy or a wonderfully juicy, fruit-driven Beaujolais. Chicken meat absorbs wine, as well as herb aromas, especially well.

Munster Cheese and Gewürztraminer

Munster is a soft, cow's milk cheese which has a washed rind and a rustically savory and slightly tart taste. The smell; smooth, soft consistency; and smeary red rind are characteristic of this cheese. Expertly matured Munster tastes mild, but intense. Gewürztraminer, with a touch of residual sweetness, is an especially good accompaniment because of its milder acidity, higher alcohol and expressive aromas (yellow plum, ripe apricot, rose petal and marzipan). These qualities are ideal complements to the spicy creaminess and saltiness of Munster.

Cheese Fondue and Fendant

Melted Alpine cheeses (e.g., Vacherin, Greyerzer, Appenzeller), Fendant du Valais, a shot of Kirsch and a hearty, crusty bread which absorbs this rich mass? Delicious! A Fendant du Valais is a mild, low-acid, dry, white wine made from the white grape variety Chasselas (Gutedel). It should show distinct mineral notes in order to accompany a cheese fondue perfectly. Red wine hardly has a chance, because its tannins taste bitter in combination with the cheese fondue.

Stilton and Port

This cheese has a distinct, nutty aroma and tastes, unlike Roquefort, almost mild, pleasantly fruity and savory. It is a typical seasonal cheese. The best Stilton is produced in summer, and comes to market in late autumn and in the winter months. In England, Stilton is traditionally served with port wine, or is even doused with port. This is done by pouring port into a small (scooped-out) cavity in a loaf of Stilton, after which a spoon is used to create a creamy Stilton-port paste. The combination derives its appeal from the extreme combination of savory-salty cheese aromas, and the port's intense sweetness and delicious fruit aromas.

Foie Gras and Noble Sweet Wine

The very rich foie gras is ideally paired with wines that possess an intense sweetness; concentrated fruit aromas; and a balancing acidity. It is not without good reason that many foie gras dishes are served with fruit such as sautéed apples, caramelized pear slices, fruity jellies, chutneys and compotes. Sprinkle with a few grains of fleur de sel and serve with fruit bread for additional enhancement. This alliance creates an exquisite taste explosion and can become dangerously addictive.

Entrecôte and Bordeaux

Several grape varieties are usually blended when making a Bordeaux wine: depending on the area there is usually a high proportion of Cabernet Sauvignon, Merlot, Cabernet Franc and/or small amounts of Petit Verdot and/or Malbec. Especially in their youth, these wines contain a considerable amount of tannin as well as robust bell pepper, cassis and strong barrique notes. The intense roasted aromas (umami) from the seared and roasted meat help to soften the astringent, seemingly harsh tannins of a young, red Bordeaux, thereby allowing the youthful fruit aromas to come to the fore. With this combination, even a closed or inaccessible Bordeaux develops into a fascinatingly delicious wine, leaving you to crave the next glass.

Choucroute and Alsatian Riesling

This opulent dish is made of mild cooked sauerkraut, onions, meat, bacon and sausages which have a high fat-content. The wine that can withstand this substantial combination needs to have minerality, fruit, substance and a certain amount of acidity in order to absorb the fat. This dish is specially tailored for profound, opulent Alsatian Riesling wines.

Beef Bourguignon and Pinot Noir

This is a wonderful stew which appears to have been created especially for Pinot Noir. First, the meat is seared, allowing roasted aromas to develop. These aromas are then softened during the stewing process. The added root vegetables, celery, onions and carrots create a thick, slightly sweet stew sauce which lets the Pinot Noir appear pleasantly fruity while integrating the acidity. Certainly a food and wine match made in heaven.

Tip: try switching wine partners. You'll see: a Bordeaux will lose its expressive fruit when paired with the boef bourguignon's soft-roasted and lightly sweet, stewed aromas. The wine will become unpleasantly dusty and tannic. The elegant, rather acidic Pinot Noir will clash with the slightly bitter roasted notes of the entrecôte. The wine's fruit will change unfavorably into ripe, strawberry-like aromas and the Pinot Noir will become boring and soft.

Meat and Wine Everyone has heard this alleged rule of thumb before: it is not the color of the meat, but the way it is prepared which provides the necessary information about the right choice of wine and its color. Cooked or poached meat most often goes well with white wine, while barbecued, grilled, roasted or braised meat is a better match with red wine. This process of roasting or searing creates a crust and distinct roasted aromas (known as the Maillard Reaction, see page 97) these find a harmonious kinship with a red wine's tannins.

Fish and Wine Exceptions prove the rule. On this principle, the above statement about the importance of meat preparation methods unfortunately cannot be applied to fish. Fish protein and powerful red wine-tannins don't get along very well. However, when fish is grilled or roasted, a light-red wine could be brought into play thanks to the Maillard Reaction. Light, fruity red wines usually have low tannin levels and seem similar in taste to a white wine. Since fish is more or less neutral in taste, the choice of wine particularly depends on the sauce and the side dishes.

Roast Goose and Pinot Noir The best wine to pair with a fatty, roast goose with a crispy skin is a youthful, fresh and fruity Pinot Noir. For this combination one needs a wine with tannins, fruit aromas, vivacity and, most of all, acidity. The wine should complement the goose and all its side dishes, and whet one's appetite for the next bite. Imagine a powerful, alcoholic Australian Shiraz. With this wine, the goose would not go down well.

Rich, Cream-based Sauces and Wooded Chardonnay A barrique-aged Chardonnay can really score points in combination with creamy, butter-based sauces. The same is true for pasta with rich sauces with a high fat-content. With the wine's creamy structure, it completely absorbs the fat-content in the sauce–and its alcohol is buffered by the fat.

Mushrooms and Wine With mushrooms, it's wonderfully easy to bridge gaps between certain wine types. When mushrooms are in a cream-based sauce, then almost any barrique-aged Chardonnay will be a friendly match. If the mushrooms are part of a meat dish and a hearty sauce, then one can pair this with mature, red wines which show earthy notes reminiscent of the forest floor.

Vegetables and Wine The majority of vegetables generally serve wine well as a catalyst. Almost all vegetables can buffer extreme wine components (e.g., sweetness, acidity, bitterness) as well as build bridges between the respective components. Cucumber, for example, is an excellent catalyst for Sauvignon Blanc; asparagus gives low-acid wines more character; and braised vegetables buffer acidity.

Potatoes and Wine Side dishes made of potatoes (but also legumes, rice and pasta) serve as absolute acid buffers. The starch thoroughly absorbs a young wine's acidity and makes it smooth.

Acidity and Wine Young, fresh, fruity wines–with and without tannins–can definitely have problems with acidity in food. When combined correctly, acidity is indeed capable of emphasizing a wine's fruity aromas. Just think of oysters with lemon juice, paired with a Muscadet. Alternatively, an apple tart with lots of fruit acidity and a caramelized crust can transform an overripe Riesling into a crisp, fruity and youthful wine. Before conducting such counteracting experiments, they should be put to the acid test. Theoretical knowledge is not enough.

Hot Spices and Wine When using hot spices (e.g., curry and chili) of most importance is not the preparation method or the type of meat, but the degree of heat the spice has. As a general rule, wines with a fine fruit-acidity interplay, low alcohol and natural residual sweetness are an excellent match. The more persistent the spice, the more intense the wine's sweetness should be. A word of caution: conversely, a dry, high-alcohol wine will exponentiate the spicy heat.

Asian Cuisine and Wine The individual Asian cuisines rely mainly on the dominant taste of spices and make use of salty, sweet or spicy marinades. Its excitement lies in the contrasting characteristics of saltiness, spiciness and sweetness. For this reason, wines with a refreshing and lively balance between fruit, sweetness and acidity–such as Riesling–are excellent matches. Depending on their residual sweetness levels, these wines are capable of enhancing and highlighting exotic aromas (e.g., ginger, lemongrass, mango and coriander). In the process, the wine's character barely changes. Its sweetness is absorbed and offset by the hot spice while the acidity bonds with the salt, triggering a taste explosion. This, in turn, has the consequence that sweet wines can–depending on acidity, salt and spice in the food–taste almost fruity and dry.

Bread and Wine Every wine lover is familiar with the delicious combination of bread and wine, two ingredients which are mutually enhancing. Each tastes good on its own, but as a team this combo is unbeatable. Bread is made of flour, yeast and/or sourdough, water, and salt. Its crunchy crust delivers toasty aromas and, depending on the type of flour, its interior is lush pale to savory dark. Furthermore, it contains carbohydrates and starch which, in connection with saliva, tastes faintly sweet and has a neutralizing-to-stimulating effect on acidity, tannin, alcohol, etc.

Cheese and Wine Cheese is one of the most important foods made of milk. It contains almost all of the milk's nutrients in concentrated form. The traditional, universal rule always associates red wine and cheese. But this is a false notion, for there are very few cheeses which actually pair well with red wine. This stems from the problematic relationship between the cheese's lactoprotein derivatives and the red wine's tannins. There is also the high salt content which, depending on the cheese variety, is clearly a better match with white wine (preferably with some sweetness and fine acidity).

Dessert and Wine Dry wines, especially dry sparkling wines with CO_2, are not compatible with sweet desserts. As a general rule, the sweetness of a wine must be more intense than the dessert's sweetness. A dessert is, for the most part, made of many wine-adverse ingredients (e.g., fruit, chocolate, sugar and ice cream). Hence fruity, rich sweet wines are better matches than delicate late-harvest Rieslings. But pairing wine with dessert is always a balancing act: when the dessert's sweetness is too extreme to the taste and there is little or no balancing acidity, then it will become a massive, nearly insurmountable wall.

Quick Finder: Who with Whom?

Dish / Food	Wine Description	Wine	Wine Type
Antipasti (grilled vegetables)	Uncomplicated, fruity, harmonious white wines and light rosé wines	Vernaccia di San Gimignano Rosé	White Wine Type 2 Red Wine Type 1
Apple tart	White wine, sweet, mature, not too much acidity	Riesling mature	Sweet Wine Type 2, 3
Oysters	White wine, minerally, fresh, fruity	Muscadet, Chablis	White Wine Type 1, 2, 3
Chicken, roasted	White wine, fruity, juicy, elegant, with smooth texture or red wine, fruity, medium-bodied, low tannin level	Riesling Großes Gewächs, Pinot Noir	White Wine Type 3 Red Wine Type 2
Bread	Generally suitable for all wines		
Camembert	Red wine, medium-bodied, elegant, stimulatingly fruity	Pinot Noir, St. Émilion	Red Wine Type 2, 3
Carpaccio of beef	Red wine, medium-bodied, fruity	Chianti	Red Wine Type 2
Coq au Vin	Red wine, medium-bodied, fruity	Beaujolais, Pinot Noir	Red Wine Type 2
Sausage with curry ketchup	Opulent red wines with more alcohol and fruit sweetness	Roussillon, Châteauneuf-du-Pape, Shiraz	Red Wine Type 4
Duck with stir-fried (wok) vegetables, "sweet-sour"	Juicy complex Riesling with structure and body	Riesling Großes Gewächs	White Wine Type 3
Strawberries	Sparkling wine, tingling and harmonious	Champagne	Sparkling Wine Type 2
Fish, pan-fried or grilled with a cream-based sauce	White wine, medium-bodied, smooth-textured, oak, roasted notes	Weißburgunder, Grüner Veltliner, Sauvignon Blanc, Oaked Chardonnay	White Wine Type 2, 3, 4
Fish poached with vegetables	White wine, fruity, quaffable, delicately smooth-textured, not aged in oak	Godello, Vinho Verde, Cru Sauvignon Blanc	White Wine Type 2, 3
Meat, stewed	Red wine, fruity, animating acidity, mature, multilayered, elegant	Pinot Noir, Barolo	Red Wine Type 2, 3
Meat, pan-fried	Red wine, young, abundant tannins, roasted notes	Bordeaux, Red wines from the Douro	Red Wine Type 2, 3, 4
Goose, roasted	Red wine, fruity, young, lively acidity, elegant	Pinot Noir	Red Wine Type 2, 3
Foie gras	White wine, sweet, multilayered	Riesling Auslese, Sauternes	Sweet Wine Type 3, 4
Mushrooms, sautéed with cream sauce	White wine, powerful, oak notes, elegant or opulent	Oaked Chardonnay	White Wine Type 2 White Wine Type 4
Mushrooms, sautéed with dark gravy (meat based)	Red wine, fruity, mature, multilayered	Pinot Noir, Barolo, Rhône, Ribera del Duero	Red Wine Type 2, 3
Chicken fricassee	White wine, medium-bodied, fruity, not too much acidity	Pinot Gris, Grüner Veltliner, Fendant	White Wine Type 2
Lasagna	White wine, fruity, harmonious, medium-bodied	Pinot Grigio, Silvaner	White Wine Type 2
Lamb curry (slightly spicy)	Opulent white wine and red wines with detectible alcohol and fruit sweetness	Condrieu, Roussillon, Châteauneuf-du-Pape, Priorat	White Wine Type 4 Red Wine Type 4
Lamb curry (hot spice)	Delicately fruity sweet wines with low alcohol and balanced residual sweetness (the spicier the dish, the higher the residual sugar)	Riesling Auslese	Sweet Wine Type 3
Lamb chops, grilled	Red wine, fruity, medium-bodied to powerful, tannic	Bordeaux, Red wines from the Douro, Nero d'Avola, Toro	Red Wine Type 2, 3, 4

Quick Finder: Who with Whom?

Dish / Food	Wine Description	Wine	Wine Type	Glasses
Lentil soup with bacon	Red wine, fruity, medium-bodied, but also elegant, with good acidity, multi-layered	Rioja Crianza, Blaufränkisch	Red Wine Type 2, 3	🍷🍷 🍷🍷🍷
Matjes herring	Preferably with a fresh, draft beer			
Maultaschen (Swabian "ravioli")	Red wine, lightly fruity	Trollinger	Red Wine Type 1	🍷
Seafood	White wine, crisp, fresh	Muscadet	White Wine Type 1	
Minestrone with Parmesan	Red wine, medium-bodied, fruity	Chianti, Rosso Piceno	Red Wine Type 2	🍷🍷
Pasta with meat-based sauce	Red wine, medium-bodied, fruity	Valpolicella, Barbera	Red Wine Type 2	🍷🍷
Pasta with cream-based sauce	White wine, powerful, barrique	Chardonnay	White Wine Type 2 / White Wine Type 4	
Pizza	Red wine, medium-bodied, fruity	Bardolino	Red Wine Type 2	🍷🍷
Quiche Lorraine	White wine, luscious and opulent without oak notes	Riesling Alsace	White Wine Type 4	
Ragout with darker sauce	Red wine, fruity, lively acidity, mature, multi-layered, elegant	Pinot Noir, Barolo	Red Wine Type 3	🍷🍷🍷
Ratatouille	Powerful rosés, fruity red wines with moderate tannin structure	Rosé Valpolicella, Côtes-du-Rhône	Red Wine Type 1, 2	🍷 🍷🍷
Venison, leg of	Riesling Auslese, at least 20 years of bottle age (mature)	Riesling Auslese Mosel	Sweet Wine Type 3	
Risotto	White wine, medium bodied, fruity, multi-layered, can have oak notes	Epesses, Arneis, Grüner Veltliner, Chardonnay	White Wine Type 2, 3, 4	
Salami	Red wine, young, fruity, rustic	Rosso di Montepulciano	Red Wine Type 2	🍷🍷
Salad with vinaigrette dressing	White wine, fruity, medium-bodied, lower acidity	Rueda, Müller Thurgau, Pinot Grigio	White Wine Type 2	
Salad Niçoise	Rosé or light-red wine, fruity, no oak notes (barrique)	Rosé Portugieser	Red Wine Type 1, 2	🍷 🍷🍷
Salad with sautéed shrimps	Dry white wine or dry rosé, fruity, without oak notes	Rueda, Albariño, Rosé	White Wine Type 2 / Red Wine Type 1, 2	🍷 🍷🍷
Sashimi of tuna with coriander	Fruit-dominant, fresh white wine, moderate acidity	Scheurebe, Rueda, Sauvignon Blanc	White Wine Type 2, 4	
Ham sandwich	Red wine, light, fruity	Portugieser, Bardolino	Red Wine Type 1	🍷
Schnitzel (breaded cutlet)	White wine, medium-bodied, fruity	Grüner Veltliner	White Wine Type 2	
Chocolate 30% cocoa	White wine, fruity, lightly sweet	Riesling Spätlese	Sweet Wine Type 2	🍷🍷
Chocolate 70% cocoa	Fortified red wine, opulent, sweet, high in alcohol	Banyuls	Fortified Wine Type 2	🍷🍷
Chocolate 85% cocoa	Fortified red wine, opulent, sweet, elegant	Port	Fortified Wine Type 3	🍷🍷🍷
Spare ribs	Red wine, rich, opulent, fruit-dominant	Australischer Shiraz	Red Wine Type 4	🍷🍷🍷🍷
Asparagus	White wine with lower acidity and very richly textured	Silvaner	White Wine Type 2	
Wild boar, leg, braised/stewed	Red wine, full-bodied, fruit dominant	Pinot Noir	Red Wine Type 3	🍷🍷🍷
Goat, young (kid), oven-braised	Red wine, fruity, opulent, powerful, high level of tannins	Priorat	Red Wine Type 4	🍷🍷🍷🍷

Say Cheese!

Cheese and Wine

There is an old, outdated adage which says, "Cheese rounds off a meal nicely." Just as antiquated is the generally accepted belief that the best match for cheese is red wine. This rule dates back to times when it was common practice to serve very mature red wines after they had aged for many years in the cellar. In so doing, the tannins polymerized, changing them from young and rough into ripe, silky and mellow.

In a classically French menu, cheese is usually served after the main course, and before dessert. For good reason, for at this stage its intense, mainly salty, taste serves as a buffer after the main course, and offers a stimulating transition to the sweet dessert which follows. If you now abandon the traditional path of red wine with cheese, then you're on the right track. Because, interestingly enough, most cheeses are more compatible with white wines.

Leave old perceptions behind and let yourself be guided by new, and possibly unusual, suggestions!

Cheese is a very complex food. It consists mainly of fat and milk protein. Its taste includes salty, sour and sweet components and–depending on its maturity–also savory, or even slightly sharp components. The composition of these ingredients varies, and depends on the type of cheese. It depends on the milk's origin (cow, goat, sheep) and most crucially on the level of maturity. As cheese ripens, it loses water. This results in the concentration of ingredients, especially salt, acid and fat. Therefore, with increasing maturity the parameters dictating the appropriate wine choices change. Due to the international diversity, it helps to divide the various types of cheeses–like wine–into types, or groups. The prescription for a successful combination is closely related to the specific taste properties of cheese and wine.

Who with Whom?

The first problem arises at the very beginning: with or without? This is in reference to the cheese rind which encases and protects the cheese's interior. Cheese lovers fall into one of two groups: some invariably eat the whole cheese, rind and all, while others trim every morsel so skillfully that not a single bit of rind lands on their tongue. Both are permissible. Unless otherwise specified, eating the rind, in moderation, is not harmful. The rind contributes something to the cheese's individual character. Depending on the cheese's maturity, the rind can taste so intense that it is better to remove it, if not at least partially.

What Type?

In general, cheese can easily be classified according to the type of milk it's made from: cow's, sheep's or goat's milk. More appropriate, however, is a classification into "cheese groups" according to method of production, texture and fat content.

1. **Fresh Cheese** (e.g., Curd cheeses such as quark, double-cream cheese, Crottin de Chavignon frais, Sainte-Maure frais, Robiola, Ricotta, Mozzarella and Mascarpone)

Fresh cheeses are not ripened, and are meant for immediate consumption. Predominantly produced from cow's milk, they are, of course, also made from goat's and sheep's milk. They have a relatively high moisture content, making them quite perishable. The fresh goat's milk cheeses mentioned here are specifically meant to be eaten in a fresh state, but these same cheeses are available in matured versions and are then categorized into the group of goat cheeses. All of these fresh cheeses have a high lactose (milk sugar) content and a slightly sour note, but due to their moistness they are relatively low in salt. A fresh, fruity, sweet white wine is a particularly good match because it boosts the cheese's flavor with its fruity notes. Powerful, tannic wines would taste metallic and bitter in this union because their tannins would collide with the milk protein and lactose.

2. Goat and sheep (e.g., Bouton de Culotte, Crottin de Chavignol, Banon, Sainte-Maure, Puligny St. Pierre, Briquette de Poiset, Cendre de Niort and Brin d'Amour aux herbes)

Goat's and sheep's milk cheeses are characterized by a typical, slightly sour flavor with aromas of green nuts. Most notable are their special shapes (pyramids, cylinders, cones, and disks) and the manner in which they are processed. They come lightly coated with ashes, herbs, plain, or wrapped in aromatic leaves. As they ripen, they lose moisture and become increasingly chalky, dry and crumbly. Their taste becomes more intense, savory and, with advanced ripening, even salty. In their youth, these cheeses prefer fresh, fruity wines. When seasoned with herbs as they ripen, they prefer medium-bodied to complex white wines that absorb their intense flavors well.

3. Soft cheese with a rind of white mold (e.g., Brie de Meaux, Camembert, Coulommiers, Chaource, Brillat-Savarin, Gaperon à l'Ail, St. Felicien and St. Marcellin)

The downy, white rind is typical of this wonderfully creamy, fatty cow's milk cheese. It is salted and then sprayed with a cheese mold culture (*penicillium candidum*). In addition to the milk, this mold has a very strong impact on the flavor and gives the cheese a slightly mushroom-like flavor. The fat in this distinctive cheese buffers wine's acidity, pleasantly highlights its fruit and can, in turn, even soften tannins. In addition to dry, lively and complex white wine types, fruity and more acidic reds with moderate oak notes such as Pinot Noir, Chianti, Bordeaux and Côtes de Bourg can be enjoyable in this combination.

4. Cheeses with an unheated, pressed pâte (e.g., Appenzeller, Old Gouda, Trappe à la noix, St. Nectaire, Mimolette Extra Vieille, Tomme de Savoie, Morbier, Tête de Moine and Taleggio)

This category includes a variety of cheeses, mostly made from cow's milk, which differ in shape, texture, rind composition and, of course, taste. In order to intensify the whey draining process, the dough is pressed. The lower the pressure, the softer the resultant cheese, the stronger the pressure, the firmer it gets. The cheese's salt content can enhance a wine's fruit flavors

and, therefore, has an influence on the wine selection. At the same time, it neutralizes or smooths out any astringent, bitter, wood notes. So all this makes a clear case for medium-bodied reds as well as luscious, fruity, creamy white wines with low acidity and relatively high alcohol content.

5. Soft cheese with a washed rind (e.g., Langres, Munster, Reblochon, Pont l'Evêque, Maroilles, Livarot, Ami Chambertin, Epoisses, Trou de Cru and Vacherin) The majority of these cheeses are made from cow's milk and are, during ripen-ing, periodically washed with a brine made of water, salt and red smear, which, depending on the cheese type, is enriched with aromatics (cider, wine, grappa, etc.). Washing prevents the growth of mold and promotes the growth of the dairy bacterium, which produces a reddish smear and a characteristic flavor. Soft, opulent, un-oaked or oaked wines with higher alcohol levels are just right with this cheese type. These savory, fatty cheeses are able to buffer high alcohol, absorb dry, bitter flavors and neutralize acid. But medium-bodied, fruity, sweet wines also respond well to these salt-washed cheeses with their savory, creamy interior and delicate, soft texture.

6. Cheese with heat-treated and pressed dough (e.g., Parmigiano [30 months], Manchego, Comte extra vieux, Emmental Grotte, Sbrinz, Gruyère and Beaufort) All of these varieties—except Parmesan and Manchego—come from Alpine regions and were originally produced by farmers for their own sustenance. During production, the dough is heated and pressed with great force, which causes the liquid to drain. This creates a correspondingly small, but very concentrated, cheese. An optimum quality is reached when the salt crystal-lizes out after an appropriate aging period. Due to their concentrated salt, fat and umami content, these cheeses are able to bind tannins. These cheeses are, therefore, among the very few truly good matches for red wine.

7. Blue Cheeses (e.g., Fourme d'Ambert, Bleu d'Auvergne, Bleu de Gex, Roquefort, Gorgonzola and Stilton)

This relatively fatty cheese is made from cow's, sheep's and occasionally also goat's milk. Due to the color of its interior, they are known as blue cheese. With a syringe, the fresh un-ripened cheese is inoculated with *penicillium glaucum*. The fungus grows in vein-like branches. Depending on the variety, some cheeses are also pierced with long needles during the ripening period in order to supply oxygen to their interior, thereby ensuring that the mold spreads evenly. The spores can thus penetrate into the interior of the cheese. The fungus promotes the breakdown of proteins, concentrates the salt content, and gives the cheese a creamy texture. Depending on the salt content and maturity, sweet wines with different residual sugar levels are favorable. While a young Fourme d'Ambert is content with a fruity, elegant Riesling Auslese, a mature Stilton calls for compact, rich and alcoholic wines such as Ruby or Vintage port. In the case of Roquefort cheese, harmony cannot be achieved with sugar levels below those of Beerenauslese or Sauternes. The fact is, the high salt content and fat are capable of neutralizing sweetness, alcohol and astringent components while emphasizing fruit flavors. Or conversely, the wine's sweet and fruity components enhance this particular cheese flavor perfectly.

Helpful tips for perfect enjoyment				
In order to achieve a perfect alliance between cheese and wine, you should heed the following points				
Proper Storage Conditions (temperature and humidity)	The Right Temperature for Consumption	The Right Level of Maturity for Consumption	Selection of Cheeses and Sequence of Consumption	With or Without Rind
If cheese is stored too warm, the cultures start to work causing the cheese to ripen faster. At colder temperatures maturation stops, the cheese gets hard and a bitter taste can develop. (Temperature for a longer shelf life is approximately 4 to 8°C; temperature for a shorter period of storage is 12°C; humidity at 60%)	Cheese should be taken out of the refrigerator about an hour before serving so it can warm up to 16 to 18° C. Cold cheese tastes like rubber and cannot reveal its delicious flavor!	Cheese should be consumed "au point," meaning at the point of flavor perfection; therefore not too young and not too ripe.	Always from light to strong flavored	The rind is part of the cheese and its character. It affects the taste (usually intense, sharp and sometimes somewhat bitter).

Which Wine with Which Cheese?

Cheese Type	Fat Content (absolute)	Origin	Wine Type	Examples
Ami Chambertin	25%	Cow's milk, Burgundy		Soft Gevrey Chambertin with body or opulent, fruity, higher alcohol white wines
Banon	20%	Goat's milk, Provence		Fruity Provence rosé, delicate fruit sweetness
Brie de Meaux	20%	Cow's milk, Marne		Pinot Noir, typical, fruity with soft tannins
Brillat-Savarin	35%	Cow's milk, Burgundy		Riesling or Pinot Blanc (Cru quality from northern regions) with fresh acidity
Brin d'Amour aux herbes	22%	Sheep's milk, Corsica		Pinot Blanc or Gris, not too high in alcohol but with creamy texture and fruit
Briquette du Poiset	25%	Goat's milk, Burgundy		Opulent, ripe Riesling, medium dry, with distinct residual sugar
Chaource	25%	Cow's milk, Champagne		Riesling Großes Gewächs (Cru quality from northern regions) with low alcohol and good acidity. Or Champagne, naturally!
Comté extra vieux	30%	Cow's milk, Jura		Vouvray, ripe and opulent, with aromas of mushrooms and quince, together with sufficient lively acidity
Coulommiers	20%	Cow's milk, Marne		Pinot Noir or Chianti, fruity with soft tannins
Crottin de Chavignol frais	25%	Goat's milk, Loire (Centre)		Riesling Kabinett or Spätlese, fruity sweet, juicy
Crottin de Chavignol medium	25%	Goat's milk, Loire (Centre)		Riesling Kabinett with fruity sweetness, youthful fresh Sauvignon Blanc, slightly mature, complex and elegant Sancerre
Crottin de Chavignol matured	25%	Goat's milk, Loire (Centre)		Slightly mature, complex and elegant Sancerre
Epoisses	24%	Cow's milk, Burgundy		Ripe Pinot Noir with body and not too much oak or opulent, fruity white wines with more alcohol
Fourme d'Ambert	26%	Cow's milk, Auvergne		Beerenauslese, dense and rich
Gaperon à l'Ail	24%	Cow's milk, Auvergne		Traminer with similarly spicy aromas, slightly rustic, sweet
Gouda old	33%	Cow's milk, Holland		Rustic, spicy red wine from Southern France with ample tannins and alcohol
Langres	23%	Cow's milk, Champagne		Creamy Champagne, Pinot Noir-dominant or an Eau de Vie

Which Wine with Which Cheese?

Cheese Type	Fat Content (absolute)	Origin	Wine Type	Examples
Livarot	21%	Cow's milk, Normandy		A spicy, luscious, ripe Pinot Blanc or Pinot Gris with a higher alcohol content
Manchego	38%	Sheep's milk, Spain	🍷🍷🍷	Ripe red wine, e.g., a traditional, elegant Rioja with fine tannin structure
Mimolette	30%	Cow's milk, North	🍷🍷🍷🍷	Rustic, spicy red wine from Southern France with tannins and alcohol
Morbier	23%	Cow's milk, Jura		Riesling Großes Gewächs with creamy texture and complexity
Munster	26%	Cow's milk, Alsace	🍷🍷🍷🍷	Gewürztraminer with creamy texture or other opulent white wine
Parmesan	25%	Cow's milk, Italy	🍷🍷🍷🍷	Opulent, structured Italian red wine with low acidity, e.g. Aglianico from Campania
Reblochon	25%	Cow's milk, Haute Savoie		Opulent Pinot Blanc or Pinot Gris or Chardonnay with delicate oak notes
Roquefort	32%	Sheep's milk, Aveyron	🍷🍷🍷 🍷🍷🍷🍷	Trockenbeerenauslese; the high level of saltiness calls for a sweet counterbalance
Sainte-Maure	24%	Goat's milk, Touraine	🍷🍷🍷	Riesling Großes Gewächs (northern regions) with lower alcohol and good acidity
St. Nectaire	26%	Cow's milk Auvergne		St. Aubin 1er Cru (oaked Chardonnay)
Sbrinz	30%	Cow's milk, Switzerland	🍷🍷🍷	Classic Bordeaux, complex, elegant, classic and mature
St. Marcellin	21%	Cow's milk, Isère	🍷🍷	Opulent, ripe Riesling or Silvaner with lightly spicy, earthy notes
Stilton	25%	Cow's milk, England	🍷🍷	LBV port, intense fruit, sweetness and high alcohol
Taleggio	25%	Cow's milk, Italy	🍷🍷🍷	Riesling or Pinot Blanc, Großes Gewächs/Grand Cru with good acidity
Tête de Moine	35%	Cow's milk, Swiss Jura	🍷🍷🍷	Classic red wine, complex, elegant and mature
Tomme de Savoie	27%	Cow's milk, Savoie		Chardonnay or Burgundy, barrique-aged
Trappe à la noix	27%	Cow's milk, Bretagne	🍷🍷🍷	Mature, classic Bordeaux with earthy notes
Vacherin Mont d'Or	24%	Cow's milk, Swiss Jura	🍷🍷🍷	Dezaley with minerality or Riesling, Pinot Blanc, elegant and complex

Chocolate and Wine

Delicious Alliances that Make You Melt

Chocolate has always been considered difficult to pair with dry whites and reds. It was just that, for a long time, there was a limited choice; only sweet milk chocolate and, at best, bittersweet chocolate. But the range of choice in chocolate has grown so explosively in recent years, that the chances of finding the perfect wine for chocolate has greatly improved.

The base for every chocolate is the raw paste that is made from cocoa beans (which are the seeds of the cacao fruit). The fresh cocoa fruit is fermented, and dried, and the individual cocoa beans are removed. These are roasted before they are finally ground in to a viscous mass of cocoa paste. These production processes have similarities to wine making, and also have similar effects. During fermentation, the beans' flavor precursors are formed, which appear later in the chocolate and are chemically related to wine aromas. Wines which are aged in barriques (toasted oak barrels) are often characterized as chocolaty, because their aromas are reminiscent of roasted cocoa beans. Moreover, in addition to the traditional ingredients of sugar, milk and vanilla, the rich cocoa mass can be mixed with other ingredients that support a liaison between wine and chocolate, such as salty, mineral, savory, spicy, sour, fruity and tart ingredients.

The successful combination of wine and chocolate depends primarily on the cocoa content.

Whether there are pleasing combinations depend, above all, on the cocoa content of chocolate. This also constitutes the main difference between the respective chocolate types.

Who with Whom?

Milk Chocolate

Milk chocolate has a cocoa content of 30 to 45 percent. The rest is made up of cocoa butter and milk (or cream) and a great deal of sugar. Sweet white wines with fresh acidity and delicious fruit flavors can usually pair very well with a creamy milk chocolate. If one prefers to drink dry or semi-dry white wines, these will pair better with milk chocolate that contains a dash of salt, a touch of acidity and citrus flavors (lemon zest, for example). This will be a perfect pairing, because salt acts as a flavor-enhancer and bonds with sweetness and acidity. Simply try it out: sprinkle a dash of salt on the next piece of chocolate you set out to nibble. When this composition melts in your mouth, you will be impressed by how the taste is augmented to a stimulating and delicious level.

Milk Chocolate with Nuts

Somewhat fuller-bodied, barrique-aged white wines cannot cope with creamy sweet milk chocolate. This style of wine deals better with more intensely flavored milk chocolate, which contains fatty nuts or almonds. These accommodate the wine's opulence, soften alcohol and tannins elegantly, and allow their fruit flavors to come to the fore.

White Chocolate

White chocolate is also ranked as one of the richer types of chocolate. As opposed to the brown versions, it contains only cocoa butter, which is the colorless fat of the cocoa bean. It gets its white color from the high proportion of milk and cream. This rich chocolate goes well with concentrated sweet wines, but also with voluminous, dry white wines. For this combination to work, however, the chocolate needs ingredients that give it structure: acidic saffron or astringent nuts, like walnuts or pistachios.

Chocolate with More Than 60 Percent Cocoa Content

For chocolate with a high cocoa content, a combination with white wine is usually unpalatable; bitter cocoa strips the delicate fruit flavors and pushes the acidity unpleasantly to the fore. Dark chocolate with a cocoa content of over 60 percent at first seems quite bitter in taste. The bitter cacao dominates the palate, and its tannins numb your taste buds and coat your tongue. On the finish, refreshing acidity expands across the palate and, with its help, the aromatic, intense cocoa flavor comes into its own. Interestingly, the tannins of fruity red wines with vegetal and astringent notes get on well with this distinctive flavor profile. On the palate, their flavors melt together on the finish and complement each other in delicious ways.

Chocolate with More Than 60 Percent Cocoa with Spices or Spicy Heat

If chocolate contains a fruity ingredient, or a spice which is also reflected in the flavors of the wine, perfect harmony is guaranteed. When the chocolate also contains a very small amount of spicy and exotic spices, a true taste explosion occurs. The hotter the spice content in a chocolate, the higher an accompanying red wine's fruit sweetness should be.

Chocolate Extreme - Up to 100 Percent Cocoa

Fortunately, the diversity of bitter chocolate extends to varieties with up to 100 percent cocoa mass. Purely mathematically, these chocolates can't contain any sugar—at most, a trace of vanilla. When tasting them on their own, they have an almost narcotic effect on the olfactory receptors that are responsible for tasting bitterness. Only after a while, but always in conjunction with an astringent layer, one can taste the chocolate's refreshing tanginess, which really brings out the cocoa flavor, and especially, a touch of fruit. These chocolates can only take it up with a wine that has enough sweetness and extract. In combination with a dry red wine, an unpleasant exponentiation of tannin would occur on the palate. Depending on the cocoa content, unbeatable partners would therefore include Banyuls, port wine, and Pedro Ximenez sherry. They offer this extreme-tasting chocolate an irresistible partnership in the form of attractive, lip-smacking sweetness.

Chocolate Opposition

However, chocolate also has some bitter enemies: elegant, pure Bordeaux, Chianti Classico, Rioja and Burgundy can never be on chocolate's side. Their independent nature—usually in the form of firm tannins and angular acidity—calls for grilled meat. Equally unsuccessful is the combination of red wine with chocolate milk. Only in exceptional cases, and in conjunction with a flavor link in the form of spices, caramel or whole, roasted cocoa beans, can enjoyable alliances be possible. But sometimes even these tricks do not help, and the result remains peppery, sharp, bitter, short and thin.

Which Wine with Which Chocolate?

Chocolate Type	Cocoa Content	Ingredients	Wine Type	Example
Milk chocolate	30%	High sugar content		Riesling Spätlese Sweet
Milk chocolate	35 – 40%	Salt, lemon zest		Riesling Spätlese dry/off-dry
Milk chocolate	45%	Nuts high in fat (e.g., almonds, macadamia nuts)		Luscious, opulent wines with and without oak, e.g., Pinot Gris from Baden
White chocolate	–	Contains only cocoa butter, high sugar content		Riesling Auslese
White chocolate	–	Contains only cocoa butter, but also saffron (tart), curry, pistachios, high sugar content		Opulent oaked white wines, but also opulent sweet wines with lower acidity levels
Dark chocolate	60 – 65%	Dried cherries		Merlot type, berry-like, juicy, rounded, medium tannins
Dark chocolate	65 – 70%	Aromatic spices, e.g., cinnamon flower, cardamom, pepper		Pinot Noir, not too elegant, more of a velvety type
Dark chocolate	80 – 90%	Roasted cocoa beans, roasted coffee beans, spices (all these only in smaller amounts)		Banyuls, Maury, Tawny port (oxidative styles) (approx. 50 – 100 g/l RS)
Dark chocolate	90 – 100%	No sugar! At the utmost a touch of vanilla (as a result, tannins and acidity are dominant)		Port (with higher sugar content) PX sherry (approx. 250 g/l RS)

Moments that Sparkle

Sparkling Wine Has Its Own Rules

Lily Bollinger's reply to a journalist's question in the early 1960s is legendary. She was asked on which occasions she drank Champagne, and her answer was, "I drink it when I'm happy and when I'm sad. Sometimes I drink it when I'm alone. When I have company I consider it obligatory. I trifle with it if I'm not hungry and drink it when I am. Otherwise, I never touch it—unless I'm thirsty."

When It Tingles

To cover these sparkling wine types in one breath is maybe a bit presumptuous and, above all, confusing. The sole commonality is the bubbly carbon dioxide. In the case of high-quality Champagne, these bubbles naturally have (depending on the length of time on the lees) considerably finer beads than those of cheap fizz. Besides their stimulating carbon dioxide, these sparkling wines, and especially top Champagnes, possess a multifaceted balance of fruit, acidity and sweetness, which is further supported by the tiny bubbles. High-quality sparkling wines spend a longer time on the lees, which contributes aromas and carbon dioxide, that develop during the secondary bottle fermentation. The connection between carbon dioxide and yeast gives the sparkling wine structure, promotes the characteristic aroma profile, and is distinguishable on the palate by an elegant texture and delicate creaminess.

Acidity Meets Sugar

Don't be fooled by the term "extra dry." Sparkling wines can contain significantly more sugar than you might presume. Sometimes sweetness is used to hide

Dosage levels in grams of sugar per liter, according to EU regulations from July 24, 2009 (in addition, a tolerance value of 3 g/l has been introduced)	
brut nature:	0-3 g/l
extra brut:	0-6 g/l
brut:	0-12 g/l
extra dry:	12-17 g/l
sec:	17-32 g/l
demi sec:	32-50 g/l
doux:	>50 g/l

Sommelier Paula Bosch also advises to pay attention to quality: "Some sparkling wines that have been bottled as Champagne are made from thin, lower quality base wines which are masked with sugar and are not only the cause of stomach aches, but also leave a metallic, sour aftertaste on the tongue. Basically, I think that food pairing is particularly difficult due to the carbon dioxide, especially for people who watch their waistlines. Rich, creamy, caloric delicacies, which many "bubbles" scream for, aren't everyone's cup of tea. Fine mature Champagnes generally have toasty notes, bread undertones as well as nutty aromas that, on the other hand, go very well with dishes containing the appropriate ingredients, because they match or complement each other in such a wonderful way; for example, the roasted aromas of grilled meat or seafood, dark gravy, stocks or sauces with fried mushrooms."

flavor imbalances. The significantly higher residual sugar-level compared to still wine is, however, not readily perceptible because carbon dioxide adds a refreshing briskness, and thereby helps to mask the sweetness.

Champagne and Food

Did you know that sparkling wine, such as Champagne, can be a very versatile accompaniment to a meal? Our French neighbors are one up on us, for they very simply call their tingly Champagne "wine," and also like to drink this good stuff with a meal. Perhaps one must simply say goodbye to prejudice and old rules in order to discover new and interesting combinations. The combination of caviar and Champagne is considered a classic–but in reality, it doesn't work at all. Caviar contains about 30 percent protein, a high proportion of amino acids, about 15 percent fat, vitamins, minerals and, depending on variety, salt, which contributes to the umami mouth-feel. Champagne reacts sourly to this protein-rich blend, tastes metallic and loses its fruit flavors. A white wine with moderate acidity and a high minerality would be much better.

What is Important?

Since the scope of sparkling wines is wide-ranging from simple, cheap, sweet and broad to elegant, finely beaded and polished to opulent, powerful, and mildly sweet, it is virtually impossible to establish a basic set of rules for its food compatibility. The main distinguishing feature is first determined by the quality of each product. A simple, seemingly sweet bubbly to which carbon dioxide has been added is doubtless not a good food partner. Whereas sparkling wines that are produced with the méthode champenoise method have greater pairing potential since their bubbles, which develop during secondary bottle fermentation, are finer and thus better integrated and less aggressive, with aromatic components to match.

Vinification

Did it take place in steel tanks or in structure-giving oak barrels? Perhaps the most important feature for food-pairing decisions is the so-called "perlage" (the structure of the carbon dioxide bubbles–coarse or fine, explosive, long-lasting, or persistent). A fine perlage results from extended contact with the fine lees, which also contribute to creaminess and elegance. These Champagnes are usually the best and most versatile food companions. Creamy sauces rich in fat can be matched perfectly with Champagne when it has enough substance, extended yeast contact and a fine mousse. Then the carbon dioxide is even able to handle slightly bitter, astringent flavors which come from the roasted notes of grilled fish or meat. Finally, a good sparkling wine provides a lively, pleasant mouth-feel that whets your appetite.

Acidity

Although the high acidity of base wines is almost always softened by malolactic fermentation, when it comes to possible food combinations, one should distinguish between the more fruity, freshly acidic Champagnes with a higher Chardonnay content (up to the single varietal Blanc de Blancs) and the succulent, vinous types with a higher proportion of Pinot Noir.

What is Difficult?

Never serve a dry Champagne with a sweet dessert. The result is a sensory disaster! The bubbly wine loses its elegance, becomes pallid and just tastes sour in the short finish. Why? The dessert's rich sweetness comes upon the carbon dioxide which leads to a sweet-sour palate impression and pushes the wine acidity unpleasantly to the fore. Careful also with hot-spiced dishes: too much spice takes the Champagne's soul and, with that, its finish. Richness and body are, at first, unchanged due to the sparkling wine's light sweetness, but then they break down abruptly when the bubbles kick in.

Some Notes to Wrap Things Up

After a multi-course menu, the sparkling wine's tingly carbon dioxide cleans the palate and creates a similarly fresh feeling, as does brushing your teeth, and is therefore perfect as a final "repair wine." Of course, this also works with sparkling mineral water. At this point we leave the choice up to you!

To the question, what absolutely doesn't go with Champagne, Sommelier Jürgen Fendt, Restaurant Bareiss, Baiersbronn, recently replied mischievously, "An empty glass!"

Maybe another tip regarding the appropriate glass:

Most people know that champagne coupe glasses are "out." The coupe's large surface area, as well as its shallow, broad bowl allows aroma molecules and carbon dioxide to literally dissolve into thin air. More appropriate is a conical, tapered flute shape with a medium-deep bowl which allows the molecules to slowly evolve before gently ascend-ing to the top. The higher the sparkling wine's quality and complexity, the larger the glass can be. Such a sparkling wine or Champagne, just like still wine, needs adequate time and oxygen to develop its true identity.

Refreshing Interaction

Wine and Water

Mineral water on the table is not just a common courtesy, it is also an important part of a meal. It contains minerals, trace elements and, depending on variety, more, less or no carbon dioxide. A mineral water is considered balanced when the ingredients are in the right proportion to each other, just as with wine.

Mineral water with higher levels of sodium, in conjunction with chloride, can taste salty. Sulfate-rich mineral waters can seem almost bitter to the taste. A balanced mineral water, on the other hand, has appropriate levels of calcium and magnesium with comparatively low levels of sodium, chloride or sulfate. Then it is, by nature, optimally mineralized. Minerals have a balancing and neutralizing effect on the acidic properties of carbon dioxide and let the water appear rounder, softer and more harmonious. In addition, they supply the human organism with essential nutrients which the body can't generate on its own.

Similar to wine where terroir influences its character, a correlation between mineral water and its origin, taste and quality can be made. Rock formations at the water's source, through which the water seeps, influence the carbon dioxide content as well as the level and composition of minerals and, thus, the taste. Most people use bottled water as an effective thirst quencher, others like the cool liquid as an accompaniment to coffee or in a refreshing alliance with wine and food.

It makes sense not only to give thought to your wine selection, but like-wise to the appropriate mineral water. Gerolsteiner provides exemplary solutions to this topic by not only giving information about the mineral composition of its waters, but moreover by recommending compatible wines and corresponding glasses.

Which Water with Which Wine?

The sensory evaluation of mineral water is similar to that of wine. Here too, it depends on the sensory perception of the individual ingredients and their interactions. Besides the bubbles' effervescent intensity, its salty-tasting sodium content is of vital importance. As a general rule, the higher the carbon dioxide level, the higher the sodium content, which in turn is very compatible with sweetness. The higher the wine's sweetness level, the higher the mineral water's carbon dioxide content may be. Reds, on the other hand, exhibit an extreme reaction to carbon dioxide. They develop bitter notes and their tannins become more prominent: the more bitter phenolic notes (tannins) a wine has, the less carbon dioxide the water should have. Try a tannic red wine after a proper gulp of sparkling water, and then try the same wine with still water. You will not soon forget the result.

Dry Wines

Dry wines require a mineral water with low carbonation. Because the carbon dioxide and sodium levels are very light, the wine's taste will be enhanced. The wine's full flavor can unfold because the low dose of carbon dioxide allows its freshness and fruitiness to shine.

Semi-dry and Sweet Wines

Depending on their residual sugar content, these wines favor a mineral water with medium to high carbonation. For wines with a high sugar-content, the carbonation has a refreshing effect. The mineral water's acidity supports the wine's sweetness. The wine can develop its full flavor spectrum, has a lively elegance and, above all, makes you want another glass. Note: the higher the wine's sweetness, the stronger the water's carbon dioxide level may be.

Mature Wines

These wines can be refreshed by a mineral water with a medium level of carbon dioxide. The carbon dioxide makes up for the acidity which is lost during extensive cellaring, thereby pleasantly accentuating the fruit flavors. The wine seems fresher and younger.

Wines with Tannins

Powerful, oaked white wines, and barrique-aged red wines with tannins favor only still water because the tannins' bitter impressions are greatly emphasized under the influence of carbon dioxide. When paired with still water, the fruit flavors come to the fore and gain more expression. Lighter red wines or wines with less tannin may be well-paired with a mild, lightly carbonated mineral water. What matters is how the tannins harmonize with the respective carbon dioxide content of a mineral water.

All Good Things Come In Threes

In addition to water and wine, another part now comes into play: food. Still or gently carbonated mineral waters are always the best food companions because coarse bubbles not only negatively affect the wine, but can also destroy the contrasts in the flavors of fine cuisine. But no rule exists without an exception: a sparkling mineral water, for example, is compatible with sweet wines in conjunction with rich, high-fat food (e.g., blue cheese and liver terrine). It brings liveliness to the heavy combination, refreshes the palate and "cleans" the tongue!

Mineral water: The ideal accompaniment to wine and food?

Depending on the variety, mineral water can intensify the taste of wine and food, but it can also have a neutral or even negative impact. Mineral water generally prevents an over-acidified stomach and hydrates, bringing the body's water-balance, which is stressed by the consumption of alcohol, back into equilibrium. Which mineral water you drink depends primarily on your personal taste, but ultimately on the accompanying wine type, the food's ingredients, the cooking method and spices.

	Natural (without carbon dioxide = still)	Medium (gentle carbon dioxide)	Sparkling (vigorously carbonated water)	Wine Type
Light-to medium-strength dishes (moderate fat content and spices)	Depending on fat content, the water has a neutral to somewhat palate-coating effect.	Gentle carbon dioxide has an animating effect and supports the aromatics.	Vigorously sparkling carbon dioxide influences the delicate aromas and can change the taste.	White Wine Type 1, 2 Red Wine Type 1, 2 Sparkling Wine Type 2
Mediterranean dishes (olive oil, tomatoes, herbs, spices, garlic, roasted aromas, etc.)	Pleasantly neutral, refreshes and balances herbal notes and even extreme roasted aromas.	Depending on the intensity of salt and spices the gentle carbon dioxide has a fresh and lively effect.	Intense spices, tomatoes, herbs and pungent garlic are intensified by the sparkling carbon dioxide.	White Wine Type 2, 3, 4 Red Wine Type 2, 3, 4
Multifaceted, complex dishes (more than 5 components on the plate)	A complex recipe requires a gentle accompaniment without the impact of bubbles.	Depending on the recipe, gentle carbon dioxide can have a refreshing, but also detrimental, effect.	Vigorously sparkling carbon dioxide has a negative impact and can have a bitter-tasting effect.	White Wine Type 2, 3 Red Wine Type 2, 3 Sparkling Wine Type 2, 3
Rich dishes (fat, protein, carbohydrates, herbs, spices, roasted aromas, etc.)	Refreshes in a pleasantly neutral way, and "dilutes." Highlights the wine's fruit, can balance roasted aromas.	Depending on the richness and intensity of spice, gentle carbon dioxide can be refreshing and neutralizing.	Carbon dioxide doesn't go well with overly astringent tannins. A high fat content can have a buffering effect.	White Wine Type 2, 3, 4 Red Wine Type 2, 3, 4 Sparkling Wine Type 3
Spicy dishes (fat, protein, carbohydrates, herbs, spices, roasted aromas, etc.)	Depending on the level of spicy heat, can have a neutralizing effect. Can balance piquant notes and extreme roasted aromas.	Spicy heat and carbon dioxide are incompatible. The spicy heat is intensified, furthermore it gives rise to bitter notes.	Strongly sparkling carbon dioxide intensifies spicy heat, as well as alcohol and astringent tannins.	Sweet Wine Type 2, 3, 4
Rich, high-fat, salty foods which pair well with sweet wine (blue cheese, terrine, liver paté etc.)	The water seems chalky and dull, and can't cope with the fat in the food and the sweetness in the wine.	Rich food in combination with semi-dry wine needs the refreshing effect of tingly carbon dioxide.	The sparkling carbon dioxide supports the wine's fruit sweetness, refreshes the palate and increases tension.	Sweet Wine Type 2, 3, 4 Sparkling Wine Type 4 Fortified Wine Type 2, 3, 4
Desserts (high sugar content)	Depending on fat content, temperature and consistency, this water can have a coating, almost chalky effect.	Light carbon dioxide can be "supportive," sweetness gains in vibrancy.	Intensely tingly carbon dioxide brings refreshing liveliness into effect.	Sweet Wine Type 3, 4 Sparkling Wine Type 4 Fortified Wine Type 3, 4

Which Glass for Which Water?

You will probably now think that this is taking things too far. That's right. Mineral water doesn't release any aroma which can be perceived, or even smelled. Its taste is perceived by the tongue. But why should one want to unnecessarily increase the effervescence of a mineral water's bound carbon dioxide? Looks usually play a more important part in glass selection than sensory aspects. For the following glasses, both of these aspects fall into place. In cooperation with the glass manufacturer Zwiesel Kristallglas and sommelier Thomas Sommer, Gerolsteiner designed two functional glasses, one of which is specifically designed for its still mineral water, Naturell, and the other for the sparkling mineral water varieties Gerolsteiner Sprudel and Medium.

Water Glass - Sparkling
A sparkling mineral water should first flow onto the middle of the tongue, to then be distributed smoothly throughout the mouth. This is accomplished by a narrower opening. The slightly tapered shape also prevents carbon dioxide from escaping too rapidly.

Water Glass - Still
Still mineral water will seem smoother and softer in the mouth when it flows from the glass through a large opening. That is why the glass is tapered outwardly.

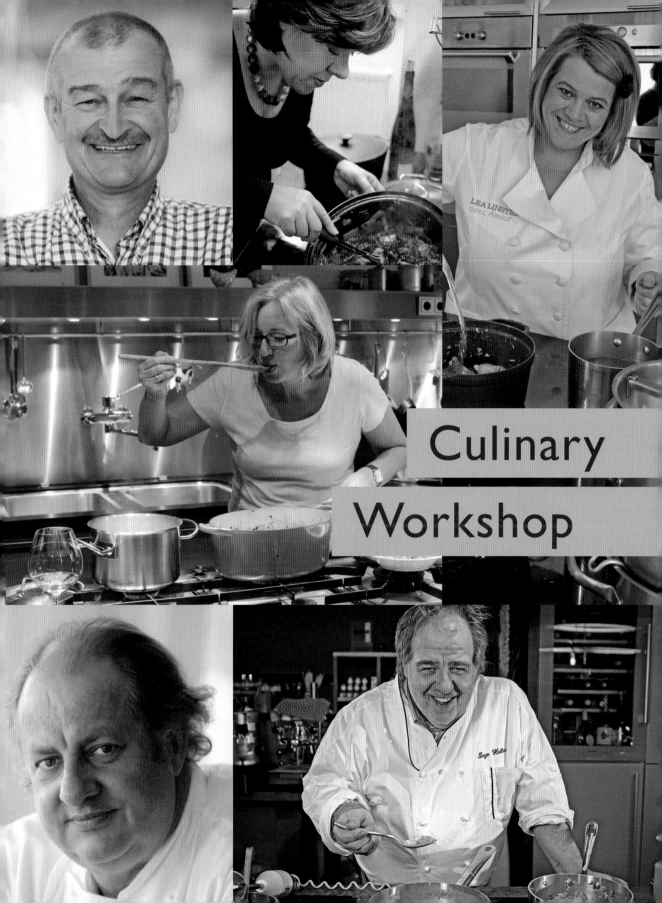

Culinary Workshop

Culinary Workshop

Our Culinary Experts' Favorite Recipes to Follow and Cook at Home

This is where theory gets put to practice. You now get to step up to the stove to cook our experts' delicious dishes. And the matching wine has already been selected, so nothing should go wrong.

.

Winemakers and chefs deal with wine and food on a daily basis, so that is why we've asked them about their favorite combinations. In this chapter they reveal their special dishes, together with their wine recommendations–a highly individual line-up of personal recipes for you to cook on your own. At the same time, these culinary experts are well aware that you can probably vary the ingredients in the dish–the wine, however, comes more or less ready to drink out of the bottle.

A sommelier, on the other hand, must–before he is even able to make wine recommendations to match the food–first procure extensive product knowledge, thus almost completing a chef's training at jet speed.

But that doesn't automatically mean that he can detect the sensory differences and, most importantly of all, also properly identify them. This skill just takes some time, patience and practice.

Therefore, it is actually impossible to create a comprehensive standard set of rules for all occasions and combinations. The topic is too broad, is a source of debate, and is moreover affected by emotional subjectivity. But that's exactly why it's so exciting and allows for experimentation. Maybe one has to only change the approach in one's own mind to lose the fear of this enjoyable wine-and-food-pairing topic. What is it about? Pleasing your palate!

This raises the question of what to do with the wine you want to drink or a wine that is in your glass when you're dining in a restaurant. Which category does it belong to, how is it made, which style characterizes this wine, and with what foods could it therefore be paired with?

Ultimately, your taste makes the decision!

Ingo Holland is one of the few chefs who prefers this particular route. He loves powerful Rhône wines and immediately begins to rave about them: "The best thing is a "Royal de Lievre" from Harald Wohlfahrt. This wild rabbit dish cannot taste more perfect – because you can drink the best red wines from France's southern regions with this dish: Henri Bonneau, Château Rayas, Jean-Louis Chave, Paul Jaboulet Aîné and some others. Everything that is infinitely dense, dark red and powerful."

The concept works well for spontaneous invitations, or when there is little time left to cook. The trick is to be prepared! Karl-Heinz Wehrheim recommends one of his favorite combinations: a young Pinot Noir with opulent sour-cherry aromas, delicate pepper notes, and slightly angular tannins to go with a sautéed saddle of venison or tender venison. "The advantage is that I can spend time with my guests and don't have to stand for hours in the kitchen, and the end result is always good. There is also a sauce that I prepare from the bones, which I save after cutting up the venison. To make this sauce I cook a whole bunch of bones with root vegetables and reduce it until the spoon practically stands up in it. Then I freeze the sauce in small portions and that way it is worth its weight in gold on such (last-minute) occasions."

Each of the following recipes serves four people. The quantity of wine is up to you. Experimenting is, of course, permitted. The range of combinations vary, thank goodness, from easy, fast and delicious to fine, complex and substantial. The sourcing of ingredients for some of these dishes fills up an entire day, however guests don't usually come until the evening. Don't be deterred, and simply get started. The wine has already been chosen, so nothing else should go wrong!

Asian Tuna and Fruity, Light Kabinett
Eva Clüsserath

600 g filet of tuna
   (sushi grade)
Juice of 3 limes
200 ml soy sauce
Olive oil
2 green onions
1 piece of fresh ginger
   (ca. 3 cm)
1 dash of Wasabi
Cilantro
Wooden skewers
Herb salad, mixed
Juice of 1 lemon
2 tbsp honey
Black pepper, freshly ground

Cut tuna filet in 1 ½ cm thick pieces. To make the marinade, stir together the juice of two limes, 100 ml soy sauce and some olive oil. Wash, dry and slice the green onions into thin rings. Press approx. 2 cm of ginger through a garlic press, add wasabi, and some toss in a small handful of washed and finely chopped cilantro. Marinate the tuna fillet for approx. one hour. Skewer the marinated tuna fillet pieces and barbecue very briefly, making sure that the inside of the fish is still raw.

Wash the herbs, shake dry, remove the hard sections, and tear coarsely. Prepare a vinaigrette dressing with the juice of one lemon and one lime, 100 ml soy sauce, two tablespoons of honey, some cilantro, freshly grated ginger, olive oil and freshly ground pepper. Drizzle over the herb salad. Place the tuna skewers on top of the dressed salad.

Eva Clüsserath's, wine recommendation to pair with the tuna:

2011 Riesling Kabinett
Trittenheimer Apotheke
Weingut Ansgar Clüsserath,
Trittenheim, Mosel, Germany

Wine Type:
Sweet Wine | 🍷

In a technologically progressive society it may seem strange that, of all people, young winemakers are putting an end to modern practices in the vineyard and cellar to go back to the methods of their grandfathers. As a young enology graduate, Eva Clüsserath's style is to look ahead–into the past. She foregoes the modern bells and whistles in her cellar; focuses on the bare essentials; and gives the wine sufficient time to develop, relying on old casks. The impressive results are already visible and, most importantly of all, tasteable with juicy fruit aromas and delicate peach scents, harmoniously complemented by a fine minerality, and beautifully integrated acidity.

The promising prospect is that Eva Clüsserath's wines will have the quality and stamina for many years of enjoyment, and will still be fit to drink at a ripe old age. Taking this step back has been worth it for this young winemaker–in any case, we are looking forward to her future. And conversely, Eva Clüsserath looks forward to the delicious union between sweet Rieslings and Asian-spiced dishes: "You don't want to stop eating because the Kabinett, with its minerality and juicy, fruit sweetness interacts so perfectly with the salty soy sauce, the sweet, honey notes and the zesty lemon freshness."

Leg of Young Goat and Fruity, Opulent, Barrique-aged White Wine

Hans Ruck

1 bunch of tarragon
Mirepoix (from 2 carrots,
    1/8 of a celery root,
    1 leek stalk)
1 leg of young goat / Cabrito
2.5–3 kg (best season:
March/April or October/
November)
1 1/2 tbsp clarified butter
200 ml ESTHERIA (dry barri-
    que-aged white wine)
Sea salt
1/2 tsp "Mélange noir"
    (a spice produced by Altes
    Gewürzamt)
1 kg young spinach
1 pinch of baking soda
3 tbsp olive oil
1 bunch wild garlic
    leaves/broad-leaved garlic
    (if out of season: fresh green
    garlic)
Freshly grated nutmeg
500 g Pappardelle pasta
Heavy cream
Butter

Wash the tarragon, shake dry and pluck the leaves from the stems (retain the stems, as they will be used later). Prepare the mirepoix: wash, peel and mince the vegetables. Do not trim the fat from the goat leg, but be sure to cut away any possible tough, tendon meat. In a cast-iron roaster, sear and brown the meat on all sides in clarified butter. Remove. Sweat the mirepoix and tarragon stems in the meat's juices. Deglaze with wine and braise, covered, for 20 minutes.

Season the browned leg generously with sea salt, sprinkle with freshly ground "Mélange noir" and return to the roaster with the braised vegetables and tarragon stems, distributing them on and around the meat. Cover and bake in an 80-degree-Celsius-oven for approximately four hours.

In the meantime, sort through and thoroughly rinse the spinach, then blanch for a maximum time of 15 seconds in salted water with baking powder. Drain. Heat the olive oil in a deep casserole dish, then sweat the washed, finely chopped wild garlic leaves (or crushed green garlic) in the oil before adding the blanched spinach. Continue to sweat the mixture before seasoning with sea salt and freshly grated nutmeg. Cook the pasta according to package instructions, making sure that they are cooked al dente.

Remove the roaster from the oven, take out the meat and keep it warm. Pass the stock through a *chinois* (a conical, extremely fine mesh sieve) into a wide, shallow casserole dish, and reduce the stock down. Add some heavy cream to create a sauce with a nice, creamy texture. Add the tarragon leaves to the sauce right before serving. Carve the meat, drain the pasta and toss it in melted butter. Arrange everything on a plate with the spinach.

Hans Ruck's wine recommendation to pair with leg of young goat:

2010 ESTHERIA
Weingut Johannes Ruck,
Iphofen, Franken, Germany

Wine Type:
White Wine 4 ♟♟♟♟

Hans Ruck tells us why the wine goes so well with the dish while he prepares his leg of young goat: "The fermentation takes place in small oak barrels made from local oak of the region of Iphofen. To make these barrels, Franzl Strobinger saws the oak into planks and stores them outside for four years in wind and weather. Barrel-aging gives the wine wonderful vanilla notes and is, nevertheless, not too dominant, but preserves the wine's minerality and prevents green and unripe wood notes."

The result: a powerful, fruit-forward wine with excellently integrated oak structure and rich creaminess which doesn't shy away from the roasted aromas of the goat meat. Quite the contrary; the wine is eager to be paired with the meat and the intensely flavored side dishes.

Sockeye Salmon with Horse-radish and Creamy White Wine

Frank Buchholz

4 portions of sockeye salmon
at 50 g each
50 g butter
1 egg yolk
Salt, pepper
Sugar
1 tbsp horseradish
Crumbs from 3 slices of white
  bread, crust removed
½ of a cucumber
8 radishes
1 minced shallot
Olive oil
1 tsp mustard
50 ml apple juice
1 tbsp crème fraîche
Lemon juice
1 tbsp wasabi paste
1 tsp honey
Sea salt

To make the horseradish crust: beat the softened butter with a hand mixer. Add egg yolk and continue beating. Add salt and sugar to taste. Fold in the horseradish and the bread crumbs with a wooden spoon. Roll out thinly and chill.

Cut the cucumber lengthwise into quarters, and remove the core with the seeds. Then cut diagonally into triangles. Slice the radishes into quarters. After this, blanch the radish quarters in salt water and plunge into ice water. Pat dry and refrigerate. Sauté the minced shallot in olive oil. Add the mustard and some sugar, and deglaze with apple juice. Add crème fraîche, reduce to a creamy mixture and add lemon juice, salt and pepper to taste. Set aside.

In a small pan bring water, apple juice, and salt to a boil. Season the salmon with sea salt. Mix together the wasabi paste, honey, and lemon juice and spread onto the top of the salmon. Place the salmon pieces, wasabi-side up, in the hot pan with the liquid, and remove from the stove. For a golden crust (or gratiné), place the pan in a pre-heated oven and grill under high heat. In the meantime, warm the cucumber slices in the mustard crème-fraîche sauce. Then arrange the plates with sauce and gratinated salmon.

Frank Buchholz's wine recommendation to pair with sockeye salmon:

2009 Pedra de Guix
Terroir al Limit,
Torroja, Priorat, Spain

Wine Type:
White Wine 4 ♆ ♆ ♆ ♆

The vines with the varieties Garnacha Blanc, Macabeu and Pedro Ximenez have an average age of 60 years, and grow at an altitude of 400–600 meters, producing very small yields. The reward is a rich, concentrated white wine cuvée with vibrant lemon and melon aromas, and invigorating notes of apple peel. Frank Buchholz's cuisine is constantly evolving. Originally oriented toward Mediterranean cuisine with regional influences, today he includes a wide variety of different accents. When it comes to the choice of wine, his motto is "the sauce must match the wine, and not the wine the sauce!"

That rule certainly isn't easy with this combination. The wine in question must, on the one hand, be able to deal with the pungency (wasabi, mustard, horseradish) and, on the other hand, be able to stand up to the salmon. This lucky find from Catalonia is perfectly suited because it has been fermented in 500-Liter Foudres, which gives it structure. In addition to subtle smokiness, delicately tangy grapefruit notes, and multilayered complexity, it conjures up a smooth creaminess on the palate, which makes this wine a perfect companion to this "racy" salmon with its hot entourage.

Stewed Guineafowl and Opulently Fruity Full-bodied White Wine
Ingo Holland

1 guineafowl, whole (approx.
  1.8 kg or dressed approx.
  1.4 kg, premium quality)
Salt, white pepper,
  freshly ground
70 ml olive oil
80 g foie gras
40 medium-sized garlic cloves
  (ca. 225 g, alternatively Ail
  rosé from the Provence)
1 bottle of not-too-dry
  Muscat or Morio Muskat
80 g candied lemons,
  finely chopped
20 fresh verbena leaves or 6 g
  dried verbena
Freshly squeezed lemon juice
Cane sugar
4 verbena tips

Wash the guineafowl both inside and out, dry and cut off the breast and drumsticks. Cut the remaining carcass into three or four pieces. Remove any surplus fat and tendon meat from the poultry pieces. Separate the drumsticks at the joint, and season the pieces well with salt and pepper.

Brown the drumsticks and breasts on all sides in olive oil, add the remaining bones/carcass pieces to the roasting pan. As soon as the breasts have taken on color, remove them from the pan. Cut the goose liver into large cubes, and add them with the peeled garlic cloves to the pan. Keep cooking until the garlic cloves are golden brown and almost done. Deglaze with wine. The drumsticks should be covered with liquid–fill up with broth if necessary. Add 50 g of the candied lemon.

Braise everything covered for about 30-35 minutes. Add the verbena leaves five minutes before the end of the cooking time. Take the meat out and keep warm. Remove the bones from the carcass. With an immersion blender, purée the remaining stock with the garlic and herbs to make a creamy sauce. The garlic serves to thicken and bind the sauce. Pass the sauce through a sieve, then raise the heat to cook. Then season to taste with salt, pepper, lemon juice and, if desired, sugar. Return the breasts and drumsticks to the sauce, and cook until the breasts are just done. Add the remaining candied lemon.

Ingo Holland's wine recommendation to pair with guineafowl:

2010 Condrieu "Les Chaillées de l'enfer"
Domaine Georges Vernay,
Rhône, France

Wine type:
White Wine 4 🍷🍷🍷🍷

The average 60-year-old vines from this deep-soiled Condrieu grow on narrow terraces with porous granite, which gives the wine concentration and substance. It is undisputed that George Vernay is considered the savior of this wonderful wine region, and for this reason, many fondly call him by his nickname, "Monsieur Condrieu." His credo: to respect the terroir. Ingo Holland follows this exact same criteria when choosing the products he uses in his cooking: according to quality, season and price-quality-ratio. But most of all, his

choices are influenced by his personal food and wine preferences:
"The Condrieu's lemon-fresh note is an ideal link to this intensely aromatic dish. Above all, the wine brings the necessary multilayered complexity to the table. During the browning process, the garlic and foie gras develop aromas of roasted nuts, which are mirrored in the wine. The Viognier's lime-blossom notes meld with the delicately spicy, floral aromas of the Muscat, which was used in cooking the roast guineafowl."

Chicken Fricassée and Profound, Complex Riesling

Vincent Klink

1 free-range chicken
1 onion
Salt
1 tbsp peppercorns
1 bay leaf
150 g small mushrooms
3 stalks celery
140 g flour
250 ml milk
2 eggs
3 tbsp butter
1 shallot (finely chopped)
40 ml heavy cream
1 egg yolk
Pepper
1 dash of lemon juice
1 tbsp capers with their liquid
Butter to grease the forms

Wash the chicken and pat dry. Peel the onion and cut into eight wedges. Place the chicken into a pot, and cover with water. Add salt, peppercorns, bay leaf and onion. Bring to a boil and cook the chicken for approx. one-and-a-half hours. Allow the chicken to cool in the liquid, then remove it and strain the broth through a sieve.

Remove the meat from the bone and cut into mouth-sized cubes. Clean the mushrooms and cut into quarters. Wash the celery and cut into 1 cm thick slices. Blanch the mushrooms and celery separately in salt water. Remove and drip dry.

For the Pfitzauf (Swabian speciality similar to popovers or Yorkshire pudding): beat 130 g flour, milk, salt and eggs in a mixer until smooth, then blend in one tablespoon of very soft butter. Grease the forms (Pfitzauf, muffin, Yorkshire pudding, popover, or custard tins) with butter. Fill the forms halfway with dough and place them in a sufficiently pre-heated oven, baking at 180 degrees-Celsius for approx. 30 minutes. The Pfitzauf should triple in size. When the Pfitzauf are done baking, open the oven door, leaving them inside the oven to rest for a moment, so that they don't collapse.

Melt one tablespoon of butter in a pot. Sauté the chopped shallots in the butter, then add the remaining flour, brown briefly and add the cream, stirring well. Pour a half-liter of the strained chicken stock into the mixture, and simmer for 10 minutes. Remove the pot from the stove, and stir in the remaining cold butter and egg yolks. Season to taste with salt, pepper and lemon juice. Add the mushrooms, celery, capers with their liquid, as well as the chicken meat to this sauce and heat through. Remove the Pfitzauf from the forms and arrange with the fricassée.

Vincent Klink's wine recommendation to pair with chicken fricassée:

2006 Lämmler Riesling GG Weingut Aldinger, Fellbach, Württemberg, Germany

Wine Type:
White Wine 3 🍷🍷🍷

"I don't drink much, but when I do, I don't skimp. There are plenty of good wines in the world—so many, that I rather like to go back to my roots in Württemberg. Firstly, I'm a patriotic Swabian, and secondly, the wine has a certain power which must be challenged. What I mean by this is that the wine isn't obliging on the first sip, but must be explored sip for sip. On a subjective level, it tastes better and better to me with every sip. In other words: it is the opposite of a crowd-pleasing designer wine." Vincent Klink makes this comment with a smile, and in the knowledge that this complex Riesling will not only accept his chicken fricassée as its culinary counterpart, but it will also luxuriate in it.

Stewed Veal with Tarragon and Precise Pinot

Monika Fürst

800 g veal (neck or breast)
Butter
2 shallots
1 bay leaf
Salt
Pepper
Mélange blanc spice mix
  (Altes Gewürzamt)
Pinot Blanc
Vegetable broth
Veal stock
Heavy cream
Fresh tarragon
1 lemon

Cut veal into large cubes. Slowly and gently, brown in butter in a roasting dish. Add chopped shallots and the bay leaf. Brown all the ingredients lightly and season with pepper, salt and the mélange blanc spice.

Deglaze with Pinot Blanc. Fill the pan with vegetable broth, veal stock and cream. Add a few sprigs of tarragon and a slice of lemon rind. The meat should just be covered with the liquid.

Braise the meat in the covered roasting dish in a pre-heated 160 degree-Celsius-oven for approx. 90 to 100 minutes.

Monika Fürst's wine recommendation to pair with veal:
2007 Weißer Burgunder "R"
or
2006 Klingenberger Spätburgunder

Weingut Rudolf Fürst, Bürgstadt, Franken, Germany

Wine Type:
White Wine 4
or Red Wine 3

The area around Klingenberg is one of the oldest German red-wine regions, and is ideal for growing Burgundy varieties because of its soils and mild climate. Over 10 years ago, Paul Fürst and his son Sebastian purchased a vineyard within Klingenberg's best parcels. The Spätburgunder ages in barriques whereby 40% are new. Here, alongside the Burgundian-styled Centgrafenberg Spätburgunder, wines of noble character are now emerging that radiate elegance, complexity, depth and longevity. "The cellar is only capable of preserving what the vineyard delivers" is Sebastian's uncompromising quality philosophy, which his father passed along to him. With this statement he makes it clear that good wines grow in the vineyard and cannot be significantly improved in the cellar. His mother, Monika, also relies on clear principals in her cooking: "The wine should never overpower the food." The men in the family know this, for while she is busy cooking, their mission is to choose the ideal wine to match the food. The final selection depends on the preparation method the primary flavor elements and the seasoning. "If the veal stew tastes rather acidic because of its preparation with wine and lemon, then a Pinot Blanc 'R' will be the best match. If it is more creamy and soft, then the wine should be a fine, feminine Klingenberger Spätburgunder because its pronounced fruit can stand up to the stew's power without drowning out the veal's delicate flavor."

Pike Perch Fillet and Charming, Dry Riesling
Lea Linster

2 small onions
1 garlic clove
Salt
Olive oil
100 ml Riesling
100 ml stock (preferably
   clam stock, alternatively
   vegetable or chicken stock)
Baguette
Butter
1 tsp freshly chopped
   Italian parsley
2 tsp finely ground
   white bread crumbs
2 tsp finely grated
   Parmesan cheese
100 ml heavy cream
Lemon juice
Freshly grated nutmeg
4 ready-to-cook pike perch
   fillets of 180 g/each
8 medium-sized potatoes
Sea salt
Thinly shaved Parmesan

Peel and finely chop the onions. Peel the garlic clove, remove the germ and blanch for two minutes in boiling salt water. Chill down immediately in ice water. Gently sauté the chopped onions and garlic in two tablespoons of olive oil. Next, add 3 to 4 tablespoons of water and boil down. Add Riesling, a dash of salt, and the stock, and let the sauce simmer, covered, for 30 minutes. Then purée well in a mixer, pass through a hair sieve, and set aside. Whip the cream and aromatize with salt, lemon juice and nutmeg.

Take the baguette, cut four thin slices at an angle, and spread them very lightly with clarified butter. Place the slices on a baking sheet lined with parchment paper. Cover with a second baking sheet, place in a pre-heated 180 degree-Celsius-oven and roast until light brown for 10 minutes. Combine chopped parsley with the bread crumbs and grated Parmesan.

Wash the pike perch fillets and pat dry. Melt butter in a hot non-stick pan, salt the fillets and place them with the skin side down and fry until crisp. Then, to finish cooking, place for 2 to 3 minutes in a 180 degrees-Celsius pre-heated oven.

In the meantime, cook the potatoes in salted water, then peel and quarter them. While they're still hot, place the potatoes in a pre-warmed bowl and drizzle them with olive oil. Immediately season with sea salt and mash coarsely with a sturdy fork, leaving chunks of potato. Then plate up the mashed potatoes onto pre-warmed plates, and garnish with some shaved Parmesan. Place the pike perch on top with the skin-side down. Heat the sauce and fold in one to two tablespoons of cream without mixing. Drizzle sauce around the fillets, and top each one with one teaspoon of cream. Spread the parsley-parmesan mixture onto the toasted baguette slices, and place one on each pike perch fillet.

Lea Linster's wine recommendation to pair with pike perch:

2011 Koeppchen Riesling "Sélectionné avec amour par Léa Linster"
Domaine Alice Hartmann, Wormeldange, Luxembourg

Wine Type:
White Wine 2 🍷🍷

"Dreams are fulfilled by saving up (for) those saved wishes," says Lea Linster with a wink, as she serves pike perch with, "the Riesling, that's also in the sauce."
Lea Linster is a professed fan of Riesling. Several years ago she conceived a joint Riesling project together with one of the most venerable wineries in Luxemburg, Domaine Alice Hartmann. The grapes for this selection come from the top appellation Koeppchen. "This Riesling is like me—dry, but very charming!" beams the Grande Dame. "This expressive Riesling interacts harmoniously with the pike perch, and its exotic aromas are able to run wild. The zesty acidity ensures that the wine, with its delicate bite, delivers excitement and, most of all, it creates the desire to reach for another glass."

Grilled Fillet of Sole in Brown Butter and Juicy, Elegant White Wine

Bart de Pooter, Pastorale

1 large sole, approx. 1.2 kg
1 tbsp transglutaminase
powder
50 g lightly browned liquid
butter which has been
passed through a cloth
(Beurre Noisette)
Fleur de sel
Freshly ground pepper
500 g parsley root
5 peeled chestnuts
Juice and grated rind of
a lemon
Fleur de sel
1 bunch wild watercress
1 tbsp butter
Nutmeg, freshly ground

Parsley Root Brittle
300 g parsley root
30 g rice flour
50 g isomalt
50 g egg white
2 g salt
10 g hard wheat flour

For the brittle, cook the parsley root in a 150 degree-Celsius-oven for a good 40 minutes. Mix with the remaining ingredients in a Thermomix machine, and spread the mixture onto a silicon baking mat. Bake for eight minutes in a pre-heated 150 degree-Celsius-oven and then dry in an Easydry machine.

Fillet the sole. Sprinkle the fillets with the transglutaminase powder, lay one on top of the other, and wrap tightly in plastic wrap. Let stand for one hour. Then remove from wrap and lightly grill. Cut the fillets in half, and place in a plastic bag with 50 grams of beurre noisette and vacuum seal. Steep at 52 degrees-Celsius in a double boiler for six minutes. Remove, season with fleur de sel and freshly ground pepper.

Brunoise (dice into fine cubes) the parsley root and chestnuts, and braise in a pan with some beurre noisette. Season to taste with ground lemon rind, some lemon juice and salt.

Save several watercress leaves and stems for garnish. Blanch and purée the remaining watercress. Season with one tablespoon fresh butter and freshly ground nutmeg before serving.

Bart de Pooter's
wine recommendation for the
fillet of sole:

2008 Riesling Terra Montosa
Weingut Georg Breuer,
Rüdesheim, Rheingau, Germany

Wine Type:
White Wine 2

The various ingredients of this dish, together with the unique cooking and preparation techniques, call for a relatively complex wine. Terra Montosa impresses with a delicate maturity, refreshing minerality and delicious complexity. Lively peach flavors and an almost salty-tasting acidity blend harmoniously to form a pleasant depth as well as a delicious, creamy texture which remains long on the palate. In this juicy, elegant Riesling terroir blend, the grapes from the different soils of the stony Rüdesheimer Berg (a hillside with schist and Taunus quartzite) and the slightly lower Rauenthaler Lagen (loam and loess) are combined. Needless to say, Terra Montosa does not have the dominant style of a Berg Schlossberg or Nonnenberg, but it harmoniously combines all the positive attributes of these vineyards, and thanks to its pleasant maturity, it can take on the sole without difficulty.

Iberian Pork with Anchovy-Olive Tapenade and Multilayered Elegant Sherry

André Siebertz

400 g Iberian pork loin
Juice of 8 oranges
Zest of 1 orange
60 g pine nuts
5-6 coffee beans
100 ml veal jus
1 zucchini
Salt, pepper
Olive oil
Tapenade of black
    "Aragon" olives and
    anchovies

First, score the Iberian pork loin's outer layer of fat. Sear and brown the meat at high heat, and then cook gently at 75 degrees-Celsius in a pre-heated oven for approximately one-and-a-half hours. The meat is done when it reaches an internal temperature of 57 degrees-Celsius.

Juice the oranges and remove the orange peel with a vegetable peeler, then placing the peel into the juice. Bring the juice (with peel) to a boil, and reduce to one-third of the original volume. Toast the pine nuts and set aside. Grind the coffee beans to a fine powder with a mortar and pestle, and mix a small amount into the tapenade. Aromatize the veal jus with a small amount of the orange juice reduction, ensuring that the sauce doesn't get too thin. Cut the zucchini into slices, and grill them in a grill pan. Season with salt and pepper, then marinate with some olive oil.

Let the Iberian pork loin stand for a short while before seasoning it with salt, freshly ground pepper, and the coffee powder. Following this, slice and arrange the pork on top of the grilled zucchini slices. Coat with jus and olive-anchovy tapenade, and sprinkle with roasted pine nuts.

André Siebertz's wine recommendation to pair with Iberian pork:

Palo Cortado de Jerez (Solera matured by Vides 1/56) Lustau Almacenista, Jerez de la Frontera, Spain

Wine Type:
Fortified Wine Type 3

An expressive sherry that possesses a lively freshness; aromas of ripe apricots; stimulating tangy kumquats; soft mocha notes; and elegant creaminess. This alcohol heavyweight needs a food partner with savory and spicy notes, a good amount of fat, and a high salt-content. The ingredients in this dish have the intensity needed to push the charming fruit flavors of this Palo Cortado into the spotlight. The perfect buffer, in this case, is the tapenade of black olives, anchovies and capers, and the delicate mocha flavor from the ground coffee beans. There are also hints of toasted pine nuts and roasted aromas of grilled zucchini, both which, at least at a sensory level, absorb the tannins of the Palo Cortado and off-set the alcohol. Another, complementary aromatic link is the reduced orange juice, which is found in the jus. This ingredient enhances the sherry's fruity side, and adds extra liveliness. The goal is to achieve a tasty synergy between the dish and the sherry, allowing the high-alcohol wine to appear refreshing and, because of this, whetting the appetite for the next bite.

Oven-braised Leg of Wild Boar with Red Cabbage a la King Ludwig

Karl-Heinz Wehrheim

1 leg of wild boar (ca. 2 kg)
300 ml each of veal
and game stock
1 bottle red wine
10 garlic cloves
1 piece of ginger (ca. 1–1,5 cm)
2 tbsp honey
3 tbsp prune jam
1 bunch of root vegetables
(1/8 celeriac, 2 carrots, 1 leek,
1 onion)
7 cloves
5 juniper berries
2 bay leaves
2 tbsp clarified butter
1–2 pieces of chocolate
(80% cocoa)
500 g red cabbage
Olive oil
100 ml vegetable broth
Balsamic vinegar
Salt, pepper

The meat is marinated in a mixture of veal and game stock as well as red wine for two days. Use a mild, red wine with low acidity so that the sauce doesn't get too sour after it's been reduced. Add 10 garlic cloves, peeled and chopped ginger, 1 tablespoon of honey, 3 tablespoons prune jam as well as the cleaned and washed root vegetables to this marinade. Fill a tea strainer with 5 cloves, juniper berries and bay leaves, and place it in the mixture so that it can be easily removed during the braising process.

Remove the meat from the marinade after two days and brown it on all sides in clarified butter, to close the pores. Then place it back in the pot with the marinade. The roast should be covered by at least two-thirds of the liquid. Place the covered pot for approx. 30 minutes in a pre-heated 220 degrees-Celsius oven. After 30 minutes reduce the heat to 150 degrees-Celsius and braise the meat for several hours (one hour per kilo). The meat's tenderness can be checked with a fork whenever necessary. The meat can't really dry out because it's covered by liquid. Once the meat begins to fall apart, remove it carefully from the liquid and keep it warm, wrapped in aluminum foil. Strain the sauce, reduce it strongly and season to taste. Add a small piece of chocolate (80% cocoa) to give the sauce the final touch!

Red cabbage is the ideal accompaniment. Strip off the red cabbage leaves and tear them coarsely. Sauté them in a pan in olive oil, stirring constantly. Add 1 tablespoon honey, 2 cloves, 100 ml broth as well as some balsamic vinegar to the red cabbage. Cover and simmer gently until the cabbage is done. Remove the lid and boil away the broth. Season with salt and pepper.

Karl-Heinz Wehrheim's wine recommendation to pair with leg of wild boar:

2004 Kastanienbusch
Spätburgunder Großes
Gewächs
Weingut Dr. Wehrheim,
Birkweiler, Pfalz, Germany

Wine Type :

Red Wine Type 3 ♟♟♟

"Preferably the 2004 Kastanienbusch Pinot Noir Grand Cru" replies Karl-Heinz Wehrheim, while he carves the meat with great pleasure, "because this wine now has the ideal maturity level, has a velvety depth and smells of freshly picked ripe berries. All this coupled with the Pinot Noir's acidity makes the wine appear virtually wild and headstrong, making it the optimal match for wild boar from the Kastanienbusch."

Bentheim Pork and Off-dry, Subtly Mature Riesling

Harald Rüssel

120 g pork belly
120 g pork neck
Salt, pepper
180 g pork chop
30 g vegetable oil
5 sprigs of thyme
½ garlic clove (finely minced)
120 g white cabbage
45 g butter
25 ml broth
3 cl Gin
2 cl Riesling
Corn starch
4 g cumin
14 shallots (finely chopped)
100 ml veal stock
1 cl Pinot Noir /
   Spätburgunder (young)
Cooked jacket potatoes
Vegetable fat
20 g coarse liverwurst
1 egg yolk
1 tsp heavy cream
Freshly ground nutmeg

Score the pork belly, and then season generously together with the neck and chop. Next, brown the meat and finish cooking on a grate in a pre-heated 180 degree-Celsius-oven until the meat reaches an internal temperature of 56 degrees-Celsius. Finish roasting the meat with thyme and garlic.

Sweat the finely sliced white cabbage in 20 g butter. Then add broth, two cl of gin and Riesling. Season with salt and pepper. Bind the liquid with a mixture of a small amount of water and corn starch. Grind the cumin in a mortar, and sweat with the finely chopped shallot in butter. Deglaze with the remaining gin. Add the veal stock, reduce slightly, and season to taste with salt and pepper. Add the Spätburgunder (Pinot Noir), bring to a boil, strain and season.

Peel and halve the potatoes, and scoop out a hole in each half. Deep-fry in vegetable fat. Sauté the remaining shallots in the rest of the butter, then let cool. Blend with liverwurst, egg yolk and heavy cream, and season to taste with salt, pepper and nutmeg. Fill this forcement into the hollowed-out potatoes and bake in a pre-heated 160 degree-Celsius-oven. Slice the meat and arrange the slices on a small amount of Anis syrup. Serve with cumin jus.

Harald Rüssel's wine recommendation to pair with Bentheim pork:

2007 Saarfeilser Riesling Spätlese feinherb
Weingut St. Urbans-Hof, Leiwen, Mosel, Germany

Wine Type:
Sweet Wine 2 🍷🍷

Harald Rüssel's personable brother-in-law, Nik Weis, belongs to the third generation to manage his family's 40-hectare wine estate at St. Urbans-Hof. Here, Riesling dominates the daily scene. Harald Rüssel is one of the few chefs who is capable of (and likes) cooking cuisine which pairs outstandlingly with aged, as well as sweet, Riesling. And this Saarfeilser Riesling is a real wild one, fermented only with natural, wild yeast. Please don't turn your nose up, for this is just how a teenage Riesling can smell in the middle of puberty. Much more important is the smoky minerality, the stunning sugar-acid balance, the juicy creaminess, and especially the long finish. This Saarfeilser Riesling interacts playfully with the (in part) very intense ingredients in this multifaceted dish, causing a fruit explosion. The reduced, and therefore lightly salty, sauce manages to create the requisite link to the wine's sweetness. A red wine with expressive tannins would mask the flavor intensity of these deliciously tender pieces of pork.

Acknowledgements

Thanks

As I already stated in the foreword, the delicious combination of wine and food has long been an integral part of my life. My knowledge and waistline grew over time, and eventually I got to the point where I wanted to know why some combinations work, and some do not. The real inspiration for this project came from the wine magazine *VINUM*. While preparing a series of wine and food articles, I saw the urgent need to systematize my findings and experiences. There is definitely a big difference between simply chatting about the connection between wine and food, and writing about it. Ultimately, I had to get something down on paper and create reproducible results. In the process, a multitude of questions, lots of conversations and hearty debates arose. In hours of sessions and with corresponding wines, the different hypotheses were tested for taste and impact, and oftentimes repeated and re-tested because, ultimately, a logical conclusion was missing. While doing this, it struck me that most sommeliers know which combination works best, but even so, they are far from understanding why.

It is absolutely impossible to solve all these issues alone. To accomplish this, it's important to have a systematic and patient partner with whom to exchange thoughts and ideas. Someone who, even after the umpteenth question, still listens and patiently gives answers. In retrospect, this proved to be true–even the most minor discussion was beneficial! I received indispensable support for this project from my husband, Rolf. While, on the publishing end, Dr. Holger Schneider and Dr. Thomas Hauffe gave their confident encouragement for the revised edition, Erik Muth and Helena Mariscal were also there to ask the really big questions. Professor Ulrich Fischer took the time to make important corrections, and Professor Dr. Thomas Vilgis actually managed to make me keen to learn more about food chemistry. Ingo Holland, André Siebertz and Michael Kammermeier cooked patiently according to all my guidelines, while guinea pig Christine Balais tasted all of my theories with an unerring nose and palate. A very sincere thanks to the highly perceptive photographer and filmmaker Bernd Euler, and to the graphics experts Irene von der Groeben and Kirsten Wittneven for their helpful hints. But without the editorial support from Michael Büsgen, who didn't let anything upset him, all of this would not have been possible. For a good book, many wires must run together in the correct order. This much I've learned! Last but not least, of course a huge thank you to Claudia Schug Schütz for her brilliant translation work, and all the people who have listened patiently to me in recent months, and answered all my questions. My heartfelt thanks to all of you!

The publisher and the author would like to thank the following people, businesses and institutions for their support in the realization of this book:

Gerolsteiner Brunnen GmbH & Co. KG
www.gerolsteiner.com

The balanced mineralisation and the resulting harmonious taste of this mineral water emanating from the Vulkaneiffel make it an ideal accompanying beverage for wine. With Gerolsteiner Sprudel, Medium and Naturell, which each differ in their carbonation and their mineral content, Gerolsteiner can offer a mineral water to match every wine allowing its character to shine.

Austrian Wine Marketing Board
www.austrianwine.com

Austria's regional diversity is reflected in its great variety of wine types. Because of their compact style and their climatically derived freshness, Austria's wines are brilliant food accompaniments for a variety of cooking styles and cuisines from Mediterranean to Asian, from ethnic to fusion cuisine.

VINATUREL
www.vinaturel.de

Vinaturel is a specialist for organic wines of the highest quality. Here you will find wines with an authentic, natural taste which are produced with a respect for nature or according to biodynamic practices. No technologies or chemicals influence the wine's quality or taste, but only the soil, the climate and the winemaker's talent. This brings about regionally specific and authentic wines.

Zwiesel Kristallglas AG
www.zwiesel-kristallglas.com

In its 140th anniversary year Zwiesel Kristallglas is at the pinnacle of glass manufacturers when it comes to table culture, drinks and home products. It meets the high requirements for both professional as well as household use: close collaboration with top gastronomists and renowned designers, sustainable materials, and innovative products make Zwiesel Kristallglas a worldwide leading source for glassware.

Parmigiano Reggiano
www.parmigiano-reggiano.it

Christine Balais,
CB-Weinberatung
www.balais.de

Ralf Bos
Bos Food
www.bosfood.de

Frank Buchholz
www.frank-buchholz.de

Weingut Ansgar Clüsserath
www.ansgar-cluesserath.de

DEUTSCHE WEIN- UND SOMMELIERSCHULE®
Koblenz · Berlin · München · Hamburg · Würzburg

Deutsche Wein- und Sommelierschule
www.weinschule.com

DWI – Deutsches Weininstitut GmbH
www.info@deutscheweine.de

Prof. Dr. Ulrich Fischer –
Weinbau und Oenologie
Dienstleistungszentrum
Ländlicher Raum (DLR)
Rheinpfalz
www.dlr-rheinpfalz.rlp.de

Weingut Rudolf Fürst
www.weingut-fuerst.de

Ingo Holland
Altes Gewürzamt
www.ingo-holland-shop.de

Ente im Nassauer Hof,
Michael Kammermeier
www.nassauer-hof.de

Wielandshöhe, Vincent Klink
www.wielandshoehe.de

Lea Linster
www.lealinster.lu

Sommelier Union
Deutschland e.V.
www.sommelier-union-deutschland.de

VDP. Die Prädikatsweingüter

VDP – Verband Deutscher Prädikatsweingüter e. V.
www.vdp.de

Vinum
www.vinum.info

Index

Bibliography

Guy Bonnefoit, *Faszination Wein & Aromen*, Rödermark 2008
Jürgen Dollase, *Kulinarische Intelligenz*, Wiesbaden 2006
Philippe Faure-Brac, *Kulinarische Harmonie*, Bielefeld 2004
Christina Fischer & Ingo Swoboda, *Riesling*, München 2005
Christina Fischer, *Weingenuss & Tafelfreuden*, München 2005
Harrington, Wiley, Food and Wine Pairing, in: *Feinschmecker Bookmagazine Nr. 15*, Hamburg 2009
Beat Koelliker, *Die neue Hallwag Weinschule*, München 2008
Bernd Kreis, *Essen und Wein*, München 2008
Manfred Kriener, Schaumwein, in: *Der Tagesspiegel*, Dezember 2008
Prof. Dr. Thomas Vilgis, *Kochuniversität Geschmack*, Wiesbaden 2010
Martin Wurzer-Berger, Prof. Dr. Thomas Vilgis (Hrsg.), *Journal Culinaire, No 7*, Münster 2008
Slowfood-Magazin 4-2010 / Geschmack
Ingeborg Pils – auf einmal waren's sechs
Cornelia Ptach – Umami in aller Munde
Champagner Magazin Meininger – 12/2011
Falstaff Magazin – 06/2011

Related websites

www.beringer.com
www.bringer.com www.brockhaus.de
www.deutscher-sektverband.de
www.ernestopauli.ch
www.gerolsteiner.de
www.howeg.ch/Jerry Comfort
www.landwirtschaft-mrl.baden-wuertemberg.de
www.lebensmittellexikon.de
www.netzwissen.com
www.oesterreichwein.at
www.teubner-verlag.de/wissen
www.unileverfoodsolutions.de
www.wein-plus.de www.weinschule.de www.wikipedia.de
www.zwiesel-kristallglas.com

Photo credits

© 2013 Fackelträger Verlag GmbH, Köln
Design and layout: Kommunikationsdesign Petra Soeltzer, Düsseldorf / Igor Divis, Dortmund
English translation: Claudia Schug-Schütz
Editor: Erik Muth
Overall design: Fackelträger Verlag GmbH
Copyright reserved

ISBN 978-3-7716-4510-6
www.fackeltraeger-verlag.de